No Ways Tired

A volume in
Research, Advocacy, Collaboration, and Empowerment Mentoring Series
Donna Ford, *Series Editor*

No Ways Tired

The Journey for Professionals of Color in Student Affairs

Volume II
By and By: Mid-Level Professionals

edited by

Monica Galloway Burke
Western Kentucky University

U. Monique Robinson
Vanderbilt University

INFORMATION AGE PUBLISHING, INC.
Charlotte, NC • www.infoagepub.com

Library of Congress Cataloging-in-Publication Data

A CIP record for this book is available from the Library of Congress
http://www.loc.gov

ISBN: 978-1-64113-760-7 (Paperback)
       978-1-64113-761-4 (Hardcover)
       978-1-64113-762-1 (ebook)

Printed in the United States of America

CONTENTS

FOREWORD

I will never forget the day when I first met Rev. Dr. James Edward Cleveland at the Gospel Music Workshop of America—affectionately known as "GMWA." Visiting the workshop as a kid, alongside several adult members of my home church, New Hope Church of God in Christ (COGIC), it would be years before I fully appreciated the impact of that single experience on my own lifetime development as a preacher, teacher, musician, and "foot soldier" for racial and social justice. Almost a foreshadowing of how my own identities would evolve and meld over the course of my life, I was mesmerized watching the "King of Gospel" simultaneously command dozens in the music pit about tempo, while directing hundreds in the choir on pitch and diction, yet never losing focus in orating to thousands in the audience about the power (*dunnamis* in Greek) that lies within us to "do what we got to do in this journey called life," Cleveland said as best I can remember. With the band in full effect, choir in perfect harmony, and audience standing on their feet in thunderous applause, Rev. Cleveland burst into solo: "I don't feel noways tired . . . come too far from where I, I, I [repeated] started from. . . ." It was over—cheers, tears, and hugs everywhere.

Fast forward a dozen years or so. Now a music double-major (along with religious studies) at the University of Virginia, I was asked to declare at least two musical genres as sites of primary study and performance focus. Reminiscent of my first exposure to Rev. James Cleveland and the GMWA, I chose ethnomusicology as a way to connect with gospel, jazz, blues, and other Afrocentric artforms. Pretty soon, I was reading books about James Weldon Johnson composing the Black National Anthem. I spent long hours in sound booths in Old Cabell Hall, listening to recordings of Aretha Franklin's "Respect" to trace its epistemic gospel roots. And, believe it or not, I burned the midnight oil in the basement of the music library on weekends, writing expository essays about homiletical musicality—that is, the rhythmic moment central to most Black preaching styles where the preacher and listener (congregation) join forces in a self-orchestrated, call-and-response experience that not only brings the sermon (or homily) to an end, but can also bring the "dull, tired, and asleep" to their feet in reverent applause.

My senior research project sprung from this curiosity—what is this musical moment in Black preaching? What stimulates the chemistry of this seemingly organic action-reaction in church settings? And, what does it do for all those involved in it? I would watch videos of famous preachers like Bishop TD Jakes, Bishop Gilbert Earl Patterson (now deceased), Dr. James Cone (now deceased), Rev. James Cleveland, and the late Bishop Charles Harrison Mason, Founder of the COGIC, to identify and trace patterns and trends in the words, phrases, or actions that precipitated this shift from speaking to singing, standing, and shouting. In one project, I analyzed short clips of "gospel greats" like Twinkie Clark of "The Clark Sisters" playing riffs on a Hammond B-3 organ while squalling out in perfect rhythm with the audience:

> **Clark:** Let me do one thing before I leave the organ...
> **Audience:** C'mon Twinkie...do that thing.
> **Clark:** I want you to find somebody that look a little depressed...find somebody that look tired...find somebody that look lonely [sic].
> **Audience:** Talk, Twink!
> **Clark:** They just need somebody to hold them and tell 'em that they love 'em. Did you find somebody that look like they been going through?
> **Audience:** Yes!!! (cheers)
> **Clark:** Grab 'em and tell them this...for all you've been through God's got a blessing for ya [sic].

What I learned from my empirical work on Black preaching and musicality about this involuntary phenomenon is this: It is all but automatic, random, or unexpected. Though it appears to rise out of nowhere, it is the result of a far more complicated and *conscious* pattern of communication between the preacher (speaker) and the listener (audience) where the spoken word (what one says) connects with and reflects powerfully the frank realities of one's lived experience (what one has seen/done in the past) that it compels a behavioral response in the present. This instinctive form of communication reverbs from the scripture to the song, from the pulpit to the door, from the preacher to the believer, from the speaker to the listener, from the author to the reader, and *all souls* are lifted. It's when the communicator—whether preacher, speaker, or author—operates as both *educator* and *fighter*—conveying an authentic understanding of the daily struggles and social miseries that shape one's "earthly journey," but does so in a way that attaches difficulty to destiny, problems to payoff, trial to triumph, and weariness to well-doing as the Apostle Paul did in Galatians 6:9.

And let us not be weary in well-doing: for in due season we shall reap, if we faint not. (KJV)

That is what Rev. James Cleveland did in so many of his gospel hits—he connected the music and message in ways that awaken, enliven, and inspire listeners to keep moving. He made gospel music and expression part of the salvation message. That's what he was doing when he penned the words to this famous gospel standard—he was teaching us and inspiring us all at once:

I don't feel noways tired,
I've come too far from where I started from.
Nobody told me that the road would be easy,
I don't believe He brought me this far to leave me.

And in that same tradition, *No Ways Tired: The Journey for Professionals of Color in Student Affairs* represents an invaluable gift to the universal library from which we draw knowledge, understanding, and insights. This book brings together over 70 student affairs professionals, scholar-practitioners, researchers, and thought leaders who represent some of the front-line fighters for social justice and equity in campuses and communities across the nation. Collectively, they represent hundreds of years of professional experience, thousands of hours of training, dozens of ethnic identities, languages, religions, and worldviews, yet a single focus unites them: Speaking truth to power about the *real* journey for professionals of color in student affairs.

This remarkable volume is organized into three major sections and approximately 50 different chapters. Some authors, like Harold Brown, use scholarly narratives about his time in graduate school to name critical aspects of the journey for first-generation student affairs professionals of color—code switching, family ties, and social hostility. Others like Hoa Dieu Bui draw on that same courage to call out resistant cultures, dismissive messaging, and the problem of erasure. Where some books on student affairs professionals synthesize findings from empirical survey studies littered by statistics, bar graphs, and projections, *No Ways Tired* takes a fundamentally different approach casting experiential knowledge as a legitimate *way of knowing* and telling.

Through the intentional incorporation of stories, vignettes, anecdotes, poetry, and testimonios, the editors of this *truth tomb* make clear that (our) stories matter... so too do our lives, even in higher education and student affairs. Readers will be struck by the book's comprehensiveness and clarity, in my opinion. The book not only breaks new ground on the excavation of minority professionals' journey, but it crosses disciplinary silos and methodological boundaries in a way that few competing titles do. *No Ways Tired* is at once biography and ethnography, history and philosophy, scholarship and opinion, even theory and practice... but it's certainly *not* just another book about people of color in student affairs.

This written gift is a formidable collection that chronicles and documents the journeys of *real-life* professionals of color in student affairs, a professional field that prides itself on principles of belonging, equity, inclusion, justice, and love but knowingly has a long, long way to go to live out the true meaning of its creed when it comes to faculty and staff who live (and work) at the margin... or are pushed there forcefully either by those naturally endowed the power and privilege to do so or by institutional forces that systematically demonize, diminish, discredit, or conspire to destroy conscious, courageous spirits of color journeying through the world of work to create revolutionary change *in the earth.*

To all those implied or named—my committed, courageous, *called* brothers and sisters across the globe within any and all axis of social difference—I offer this endorsement as encouragement:

We can't feel noways tired. We might *get* tired some days but we must resist the urge to *be* tired. We can't stay in that state.

We've come too far from where we've started from. Think about it. Some of us from modest upbringings, single-parent (but proud) homes, poorly resourced schools or unsafe neighborhoods or countries, through hostile graduate programs and foreign policies but yet we made it. That's the story of resilience. That's the power we have.

No, our road may not be easy, but it will be worth it. You are enough. You belong here (in student affairs). You're actually here on *purpose.* And we need you to stay.

I don't believe we were brought this far to be left out or behind. Read on and gain strength. Read on and be affirmed. Read on and find community. Read on and nod in agreement. Read on and speak your truth. Whatever you do, read on.

—**Terrell L. Strayhorn, PhD**

INTRODUCTION

NO WAYS TIRED

The Journey for Professionals of Color in Student Affairs

Focusing on issues and perceptions of student affairs professionals of color is necessary for their recruitment, retention, and achievement. By sharing their visions of success, lessons learned, and cautionary tales, the insights offered by the chapters' authors can assist other professionals of color who are new and entry-level professionals in laying a path for their success and finding ways they can construct opportunities to flourish and thrive. Their stories highlight topics that need to be openly discussed in student affairs, such as marginalization, multiple identities, intersectionality, meritocracy, privilege, social capital, discrimination, and racism. Critical conversations about the experiences of professionals of color in student affairs must occur to make the profession and discipline of student affairs better and more responsive to professionals of color. As bell hooks (1989) asserted, "When we end our silence, when we speak in a liberated voice, our words connect us with anyone anywhere who lives in silence" (p. 18). The ultimate goal for *No Ways Tired* is to provide a space for silenced or ignored voices and to promote discussions regarding how higher education institutions can be more proactive in supporting and creating environments that are conducive to the success of professionals of color navigating their higher education careers.

Even though diversity is currently conveyed as a ubiquitous principle within institutions of higher education (Brayboy, 2003; Kayes, 2006), professionals of color still face such issues as discrimination (Phillips, 2002), the glass ceiling (Cornelius, 2002; Mong & Roscigno, 2010), and a lack of mentoring and access to networks (Brooks & Clunis, 2007; Burke & Carter, 2015; Palmer & Johnson-Bailey, 2005). Building a diverse staff is important, but institutions must then consider how to retain them and respond to their unique and culture-based needs (Cornelius, 2002; Pascarella & Terenzini, 1991). Organizations that value diversity in all forms have employees with higher job satisfaction, which promotes higher levels of productivity, retention, and increased revenue (Carnevale & Stone, 1994). Students also benefit when the student affairs staff is composed of people from various backgrounds (Flowers & Pascarella, 1999). However, for institutions to address the issues student affairs professionals of color face while supporting them, they must first acknowledge that problems exist. Since White individuals often see race as less of a problem than people of color do and typically have a very different perception of workplace diversity issues and climate (Harper & Hurtado, 2007), any efforts to address race-based issues can be challenging—and they must be addressed in proactive ways.

Although the literature is extensive on the retention of students and faculty of color in higher education, literature on the retention of higher education professionals of color is limited. This book endeavors to address this gap in literature. The narratives in this book can provide a lens for higher education institutions to develop strategies and initiatives to recruit, support, and retain student affairs professionals of color.

The book is divided into three volumes: entry-level, mid-level, and senior-level. In this volume, the authors have between 5 to 10 years of experience in the student affairs field. It is our hope that readers will resonate with and understand the authors' perspectives and stories. We believe their collective voices illuminate the trials and tribulations that student affairs professionals of color experience. Their collective voices emphasize the tenacity and strength with which many student affairs professionals of color possess to effectively do their jobs and fulfill their purposes. The stories and strategies they share provide a resounding compass pointing north toward success and contentment, leading the way for those who come behind them. Predominately White institutions' (PWI) administrators and boards of trust must take time to read this book and *believe* the stories and, then, review their policies, procedures and cultural climate using the new lens they develop from these chapters; and also examine themselves to transform campus environments at all levels so that student affairs professionals of color feel supported and thrive.

We appreciate all the authors who shared their stories and most of all, Dr. Donna Y. Ford for providing us this tremendous opportunity. Her incredible drive and contagious vision inspired us.

The nearly 20-year friendship shared by the co-editors exemplifies professional and personal support, mentoring, and love. This endeavor was an inspiring *labor* of love. We hope you enjoy and are inspired as well.

—**Monica Galloway Burke**
U. Monique Robinson

REFERENCES

Brayboy, B. M. J. (2003). The implementation of diversity in predominantly White colleges and universities. *Journal of Black Studies, 34*(1), 72–86.

Brooks, A. K., & Clunis, T. (2007). Where to now? Race and ethnicity in workplace learning and development research: 1980–2005. *Human Resource Development Quarterly, 18*, 229– 251.

Burke, M.G., & Carter, J. D. (2015) Examining perceptions of networking among African American women in student affairs. *NASPA Journal About Women in Higher Education, 8*(2), 140–155.

Carnevale, A. P., & Stone, S. C. (1994). Diversity beyond the golden rule. *Training and Development, 48*(10), 22–39.

Cornelius, N. (2002). *Building workplace equality: Ethics, diversity and inclusion.* London, England: Thomson.

Flowers, L.A., & Pascarella, E.T. (1999). Does college racial composition influence the openness to diversity of African American students? *Journal of College Student Development, 40*(6), 377–389.

Harper, S. R., & Hurtado, S. (2007). Nine themes in campus racial climates and implications for institutional transformation. In S. R. Harper, & L. D. Patton (Eds.), *Responding to the realities of race on campus. New Directions for Student Services* (No. 120, pp. 7–24). San Francisco, CA: Jossey-Bass.

hooks, b. (1989). *Talking back: Thinking feminist, thinking Black.* Boston, MA: South End Press.

Kayes, P. (2006). New paradigms for diversifying faculty and staff in higher education: Uncovering cultural biases in the search and hiring process. *Multicultural Education, 14*(2), 65–69.

Mong, S., & Roscigno, V. (2010). African American men and the experience of employment discrimination. *Qualitative Sociology, 33*(1), 1–21.

Palmer, G. A., & Johnson-Bailey, J. (2005). The career development of African Americans in training and organizational development. *Human Resource Planning, 28*(1), 11–12.

Pascarella, E. T., & Terenzini, P. T. (1991). *How college affects students: Findings and insights from twenty years of research.* San Francisco, CA: Jossey-Bass

Phillips, R. (2002). Recruiting and retaining a diverse workforce. *Planning for Higher Education, 30*(4), 32–39.

ACKNOWLEDGMENTS

Editing this book has been a surreal, inspiring, and rewarding experience for us. Doing it with a wonderful friend and colleague only made the experience more special. We can certainly attest to the value of sisterhood and friendship. Maintaining commitment and stamina despite competing demands for our time and life's obstacles was difficult at times, but together, we persevered.

There are individuals to whom we extend a special thanks for their roles throughout the many hours we dedicated to completing this book.

A special thanks to Dr. Donna Ford for her dedication to and advancing research about professionals of color in the academy and for showcasing her expertise. In addition, we appreciate her vision and the wonderful opportunity to create this medium for professionals of color in student affairs to have a voice about their experiences. Dr. Ford's unwavering support and advice were essential and appreciated.

Our sincere gratitude is extended to our children—Nicole Wright, daughter of Dr. Robinson, and Evan and Kyle Burke, the sons of Dr. Burke—for their encouragement, patience, and love through all the many hours we had to give to reading, organizing, and editing.

Thanks to Dr. Robinson's former graduate assistants, Sahar Khan and Melissa Cornejo, for serving as an extra set of eyes.

Thanks to Tim Nichols for his support over the many months Dr. Robinson dedicated to this project.

Much appreciation goes to Dr. Colin Cannonier for being a sounding board and a listening ear for Dr. Burke throughout the process of the project.

Thanks also to LaMarcus Hall for his support of this project.

We are extremely grateful to the contributing authors, who were vulnerable and yet brave, for sharing their truths. Your stories are inspiring, relevant, and highlight a reality that is rarely discussed in the larger realm of scholarship in the field of student affairs.

The journey for professionals of color in higher education can sometimes be arduous as much as it is rewarding. Let us not become weary in doing good, for at the proper time we will reap a harvest if we do not give up (Galatians 6:9, NIV). Onward and upward!

—**Monica Galloway Burke**
U. Monique Robinson

BY AND BY

We are tossed and driven on the restless sea of time;
somber skies and howling tempests oft succeed a bright sunshine;
in that land of perfect day, when the mists are rolled away,
we will understand it better by and by.

—Charles Tindley (*We'll Understand It Better By and By*, 1905)

The lyrics of "We'll Understand It Better By and By" by Charles Tindley reminds us that when we encounter distress, trials, and the storms of life, we will understand the accompanying lessons in time. Lessons challenge us to analyze and reflect on meaning as well as uncover important ideas and core processes. As we progress toward our goals, it is sometimes necessary to monitor our intrinsic and extrinsic motivation, evaluate factors of influence, seek guidance, and learn to pivot. Accordingly, the authors in this chapter share challenges they encountered as they navigate the higher education landscape and the lessons they learned by and by.

The authors of the following narratives, who have been in the field of student affairs between 5 and 10 years, disclose their experiences, challenges, and lessons learned as they grow into seasoned professionals. The topics range from dealing with microaggressions, discrimination, upward mobility, burnout, support needs, institutional politics, self-discovery, self-doubt, working abroad, and counter spaces. Through their narratives, the authors' combined voices bring visibility to their lived experiences and challenges as professionals of color. From their experiences and resilience, support strategies are offered for new, entry, and other mid-level professionals to consider as the progress in their careers.

CHAPTER 1

VISIBLE BUT NOT HEARD

The Lived Experience of a Black Cisgender Christian Woman as a New/ Entry Level Student Affairs Professional at Historically White Institutions

DaVida L. Anderson
The University of Iowa

This chapter gives voice to my experiences as a cisgender Black Christian woman who was educated and worked exclusively in historically White institutions while navigating challenges related to race and other parts of my identity to be successful as a new student affairs professional. This chapter will explore the preparation of student affairs professionals, systemic challenges that Black women encounter, as well as provide practical resources to navigate the work environment successfully.

In the words of Angela Davis (Vaughn-Hall, 2017),

> Black women have had to develop a larger vision of our society than perhaps any other group. They have had to understand White men, White women, and

No Ways Tired, pages 3–14
Copyright © 2019 by Information Age Publishing
All rights of reproduction in any form reserved.

Black men. They have also had to understand themselves. When Black women win victories, it is a boost for virtually every segment of society. (para. 3)

These sentiments encompass my experience as a Black woman student affairs professional. I entered the field of higher education as a result of my passion for bringing attention to the voices of individuals who are overlooked, excluded, and devalued in society. I saw an opportunity to become a conduit of knowledge as well as an advocate for social justice and the celebration of differences.

Watt (2013) described the difference as "having dissimilar opinions, experiences, ideologies, epistemologies and/or constructions of reality about self, society, and/or identity" (p. 6). The difference for me has always been an opportunity to grow beyond the confines of my views, beliefs, and social constructions. We all have come to know knowledge from our lived experiences and formed behaviors that are unique to our personal identities. For example, when we go grocery shopping, we may purchase specific brands of foods over others because we believe they are better than other brands. I notice that I buy the same items I observed my parents purchasing for many years as a child. I have been socially conditioned to what is acceptable. However, when confronted with divergent opinions, truths, and experiences, we often recoil to our comfort zones that reflect familiar thinking. People generally believe there is one correct choice or, based on my example related to groceries, one brand is more efficient than others. This way of thinking carries over into every aspect of life including student affairs.

STANDING IN THE GAP

Early on in higher education, Black women helped fill the gap of holding student service-oriented positions (Evans, 2008; Hayden Glover, 2012). Black women student affairs professionals' presence was welcomed by especially students of color who had to navigate a hostile campus climate (Evans, 2008; Hayden Glover, 2012). Black women were viewed by students as role models (Hayden Glover, 2012) and positively influenced students to pursue careers in student affairs (Patton & Harper, 2003). Since the creation of student affairs, the field has evolved as a response to civil rights movements and the need to serve a diverse population (Pope, Mueller, & Reynolds, 2009). Black women student affairs professionals are more than just role models in the field of higher education; they are a diverse, influential movement that continues to challenge historical viewpoints and practices. Pope, Mueller, and Reynolds (2009) argue that despite the "expansion of populations, interventions, theories, methods, and approaches, individuals and institutions continue to create obstacles to further understanding of the various student groups attending higher education" (p. 654), and encourage initiatives to develop environments that are affirming to their multicultural identities. Applying this viewpoint regarding individual and institutional challenges for Black women working in student affairs is necessary.

Systemic racism persists in the United States and extends to college campuses, particularly historically White institutions due to their historical discriminatory and racist past. Jones (2000) described racism on three different levels: institutionalized, personally mediated, and internalized. Jones defines institutionalized racism as "differential access to the goods, services, and opportunities of society by race" (p. 1212). Institutionalized racism is embedded in institutions' customs, practices, providing access and power to some while disadvantaging others based on their race (Jones, 2000). Institutionalized racism presented itself early in my career and as a consistent characteristic of higher education. I noticed who possessed, maintained, and restrained power within the institution. The lack of diversity in leadership positions was not due to training or qualifications as many senior administrators were grandfathered into positions and if they applied for their same positions, they would no longer qualify based on current requirements. However, other individuals would have to meet the same qualifications for the same positions they held. Overwhelmingly, these positions were occupied by White men who relied on the expertise of other individuals.

I did and still experience prejudice statements that imply I grew up in a certain manner. Many times, the statements include a stereotypical description of being Black. For example, individuals within the institution and outside of the institution would ask me if I grew up in the well-known city projects, or sometimes I was excluded from conversations if they believed I could not relate to a certain experience, like playing the violin or tennis. I played both the violin and tennis. Growing up in my household, my parents exposed my sibling and me to diverse sports, arts, music, and culture. Consistently, I was asked to help Black students with whom the only thing we shared was the color of our skin, but it was assumed by my supervisor or colleagues that I could relate to their upbringing because we were both Black. Jones (2000) defines this type of action as "personally mediated racism as prejudice and discrimination, where prejudice means differential assumptions about the abilities, motives, and intentions of others according to their race, and discrimination means differential actions toward others according to their race" (p. 1213). This level is most commonly known when individuals experience intentional and unintentional levels of avoidance, exclusions, suspicion, and dehumanization (Jones, 2000). Being educated and working in predominantly and historically White environments, I saw or experienced institutionalized and personally mediated racism. Both factors heightened my awareness and I found myself sitting with a tension between being my authentic self and minimizing any stereotypes that could be attached to my Blackness. Internalized racism, defined as "acceptance by members of the stigmatized races of negative messages about their own abilities and intrinsic worth" (Jones, 2000, p. 1213) impedes on a person's psychological state and "manifests as an embracing of Whiteness" (Jones, 2000, p. 1213) and rejection of one's self. Internalized racism is exhausting. There are certain characteristics that all people hold but in society we attach specific behaviors or language to negatively portray another group. Doing so not only limits the vastness and uniqueness of members who belong to a specific group but reduces viewing them as a collective and not individuals due to one or more of their identities such as race or gender.

Student affairs professionals, being mindful of power differences, should encourage and promote inclusive and equitable policies and practices. McIntosh (1988) discussed two types of privilege—White and male privilege; both are unearned advantages that help them secure and retain power. These unearned advantages disadvantage groups like Black women, who encounter challenges in higher education environments despite their contributions and achievements in higher education in the United States (Evans, 2008; Perkins,1983). Hughes and Howard-Hamilton (2003) described Black women's feelings of isolation, alienation, and being ignored on a college campus by their classmates and colleagues despite being students, faculty, and administrators. This feeling could have critical implications for Black women's well-being and success. For instance, isolation can create stress from experiencing consistent oppression and microaggressions, which negatively influence their self-efficacy due to being ignored and decrease trust with their peers or colleagues (Hughes & Howard-Hamilton, 2003). Burke and Carter (2015) suggested that student affairs organizations must develop a more comprehensive understanding of how organizational structures and challenges impede on Black women's progress, including access to career networks, mentoring, and career promotion opportunities. Focusing on one of the many identities that Black women hold is inadequate.

While pursuing my masters in a higher education program and reflecting on my prior experience in higher education, I gained a realistic interpretation of what to expect working in the field of higher education after graduation. Perhaps it was my own hopes of viewing student affairs as a utopia—a group of people who acknowledge their own biases and pursued cultural competencies, and inclusion. Frequently, during my coursework for my degree, I was learning with like-minded individuals who, for the most part, did the work of critical reflection to explore their privileges and biases. Although, my faculty did a great job of creating environments to consciously confront controversial societal issues (i.e., race, gender, class, sexism, religion, ableism), rarely did I encounter conflicting thought in dialogue that forced people to engage in authentic and reflective conversations about race and gender. Even in the smallest incidents when conflicting views entered classroom dialogue, it created discomfort for everyone participating. Nonetheless, engaging in dialogue with competing thoughts is critical to learning about one's self and others. I remember sitting in class discussing sexuality and the guest speaker encouraging everyone to identify their masculine and feminine attributes. I recognize that I am naturally an encourager in the learning process and affirm individual's perspectives given that mine are oftentimes ignored. During this class period, a White male who consistently shared his affluent socioeconomic status and privilege in casual conversation stated that he, being an alpha male, felt more masculine in the environment at school but when he went home around other alpha males, he is more feminine. As he shared, his face became red and it was obvious it took a lot for him to become vulnerable with our class members. Naturally, I said softly "Thank you for sharing." The guest speaker asked me to share what I had said and I stated, "I was just thanking him for sharing." Immediately, the White male said, "I don't need your permission to share." Thankfully, I had a culturally competent and savvy professor who stepped in and said, "Let's name what just happened." I looked around the room and faces were blank, I boldly raised my hand, being one of the only Black women and said, "His privilege just spoke." This experience among many prepared me to what I would encounter in the field after graduation.

It is necessary for graduate programs in student affairs to have clear outcomes for cultural competencies and encourage continuous professional development after student professionals are working in the field (Mitchell & Westbrook, 2016; Pope, Reynolds, & Mueller, 2014). Like many graduate students in student affairs, I graduated with an optimistic perspective that everyone working in student affairs had a degree of proficiency in multicultural competency. Multicultural competence is defined by Pope and Reynolds (1997) as "the awareness, knowledge, and skills necessary to work effectively and ethically across cultural difference" (p. 270). Pope and Reynolds (1997) suggested that it is critical for student affairs professionals to not only gain multicultural skills but continue to expand their multicultural competence as they develop throughout their career.

The way student affairs professionals think is essential. bell hooks (2010) suggests, "Thoughts are the laboratory where one goes to pose questions and find answers, and the place where visions of theory and praxis come together. The heartbeat of critical thinking is the longing to know—to understand how life works" (p. 7). However, early on in my student affairs career, my thoughts and idealism of a euphoric utopia were challenged. The very theory and lessons learned during my pursuit of a master's degree in higher education and student affairs were usually ignored by colleagues who I interacted with daily. I often wondered if my colleagues took the same higher education and student affairs courses I was exposed to that helped me do a critical reflection of my own implicit and explicit biases. For example, as a Black cisgender and Christian woman, I would encounter interactions with people who appeared to hold certain ideologies that were toxic to my identities at first glance. However, I would push back against prior experiences or judgments to open myself to interacting with them in the moment to create a productive environment to coexist. I learned that my earlier assumptions were informed by my past experiences, but unfounded by my interactions with the individual I encountered.

As a young student affairs professional, I have encountered or witnessed White or male privilege. These feelings were compounded by microaggressions and macroaggressions occasionally carried out by students, and to my dismay, colleagues. For example, using culturally insensitive words or stereotypes that, given my lived experience, I could not relate to their comments, but they assumed due to my identities that was my experience. Another instance is, early on in my career, I had a supervisor whose judgment was engulfed by his White and male privileges that perpetually took away my agency as a student affairs professional. For example, while trying to rectify a roommate dispute, I took great pride in searching for the truth and fairness in every roommate conflict. Searching for truth and fairness meant for me to examine the situation from multiple lenses and include all parties accounts in my consideration before rushing to an outcome. However, I noticed over time that my expertise was oftentimes overlooked depending on the race of the student placing their complaint.

One day, a White female student contacted me claiming that her African roommate was racist against her and threatened her. Threats were never taken lightly and I gave this situation my undivided attention and designated adequate resources to uncover the truth. After following protocol to ensure that the student was not in direct harm and determined there was not a threat, I still had to speak to the other roommate before coming to a decision. Although the White female student recommended I should move the African student out of her room, I informed her that I would not render an outcome without speaking to both parties. The student then thanked me for handling her issue and helping her. However, she changed her story the next morning when her parents threatened to lawyer up and declared that I did not manage their daughter's issue expediently and complained to my direct supervisor. I shared all details and communications with my supervisor, including the communication from the White female student encompassing numerous compliments and noting how she understood that I had to follow up with her roommate prior to rendering an outcome. Given my identity as a Black woman, I crossed all t's and dotted all i's. However, after receiving numerous calls from her parents to the college president's office and our office, my supervisor informed me that he would handle the situation by excluding me and speaking to the White female student with another White female colleague. My agency was taken from me. I could not recall when my supervisor did the same with my other colleagues when similar issues arose. After the meeting with the student, I was called into my supervisor's office and I remember stating over and over that it was not fair to make a decision without speaking to all parties. Thankfully, later that afternoon my supervisor and I both spoke with the African student and listened to her side of the story. She had an accent that most people would dismiss because they would not listen carefully. After 10 minutes of conversation, it became clear that she was not a threat but instead the White student tried to disguise her own improper conduct in exchange for making the African student appear racist in hopes that she would be removed from their shared space. The problem between the two of them came about because the White student had a cat in their room, which was against school policies, and the African student threatened to tell the administration because she did not want the cat in the room. The outcome of this situation could have been worse if it was not for me listening to the still voice of justice and equality that calls me to listen to not just those whose voice is historically accepted without further investigation, but also to individuals who have traditionally been ignored. I wonder what would have happened if I was not there, a minoritized person, who understands being visible but not heard. How many times are historically disenfranchised populations overlooked because they are overpowered by systemic constraints related to race, power, and privilege? Had it not been for my presence, it is possible that this African woman would have been ignored and even myself was almost overlooked with my supervisor wielding his power in this situation. I am sure my supervisor was acting with good intentions, but sometimes good intentions leave the most vulnerable populations with a long-lasting negative influence on their development. This encounter raises the unspoken truth of our field that we must ensure our values align with our behaviors and theories are applied into equitable practice.

Good people with good intentions regularly commit inequitable offenses, which can have profound consequences against the individuals on the receiving end of the offense. The recipient of these offenses is left to salvage their professional pursuit without support from their direct supervisors or immediate colleagues. Therefore, student affairs professionals must find ways to navigate terrain that is rooted in exclusion, power, and privilege that does not favor one's race, gender, sexual orientation, religion, or other identities. Over the years, I have found methods to help me not only survive but thrive within that terrain.

BUILDING COALITIONS

I had to center myself on my purpose and create coalitions to bloom in an environment that habitually eroded my self-efficacy (Bandura, 1997;

Pajares, 1996). My core beliefs keep my focus on my purpose. As a person who holds minoritized (Stewart, 2013) identities, my purpose is also grounded in being an advocate for minoritized students who have a voice but are ignored and overlooked. Scholars advise that Black college students benefit from counter space to provide safety and inclusion for them to prosper (Howard-Hamilton, 2003; Solórzano, Ceja, & Yosso, 2000). Howard-Hamilton (2003) suggested that counter spaces are necessary for Black students when sharing their counter stories. Prospering in student affairs caused me to seek outlets and build stronger spiritual, internal, external social relationships within higher education, and family/friend support.

SPIRITUALITY

I have been guided by my spirituality to overcome oppression within the workplace as a student affairs professional working at historically White institutions. Feminist scholars have developed a body of work that reflects the connection between Black women and spirituality (Clifford, 2001; Fiorenza, 1992; Higginbotham, 1997; Mattis, 2002). Mattis (2002) suggested,

> African American women have engaged in radical re-readings of Biblical text and have embraced private beliefs about the nature of the relationship between God and humans that have helped them to disrupt and resist the impact of patriarchy and other forms of oppression including racism. (p. 310)

I draw on my spiritual roots as a guiding post to embracing adversity and others in the ways that will honor God but not give into my hurts or judgments. Consistently, I play gospel music, pray, or read Scripture before going to work to prepare myself to be in the right frame of mind as I encountered unknown and known challenges of the day.

INTERNAL AND EXTERNAL SOCIAL NETWORKS WITHIN HIGHER EDUCATION

Access and networks determine women and minorities representation in organizational structures (Mehra, Kilduff, & Brass, 1998). Working at historically White higher education institutions, I had to seek out mentors and support groups to succeed in the field. My mentors' identities have not always matched mine, but they understood the importance of applying cultural competencies in practice. They genuinely wanted to dismantle institutional barriers to help me succeed. My mentors did not always work at my institutions but made themselves accessible and provided authentic knowledge that was not always provided in the textbook. I was fortunate to have a Black woman president at our institution who role modeled, supported, and coached me on my next steps in the field of higher education. I also was fortunate to have support from mid-level administration. One administrator was a Black man, who worked towards social justice not only for his students but everyone he encountered, who was able to advocate for me in meetings that I was not privy to attending. Another person who was in my network early on was a White man who supervised my supervisor and provided additional support for my development. Sometimes you will not receive support from your direct supervisor but finding networks internally and externally will help you succeed. Later in my career, I developed sister circles—women of color who worked at other institutions across the United States. Together, we share our experience and support each other's development.

FAMILY/FRIENDS

As a student affairs professional, I have learned to remember who I am at my core. Family and friends have a way of loving you and reminding you who you are outside of the theory and student affairs profession. This recognition is important because we are just people who sometimes forget to act like ordinary people who can relate to our students and sometimes, we can get away from the human side and focus too much on the theoretical that alienates us from each other. Having conversations with family and friends about ordinary topics after a long day on the job was the remedy I needed to recharge, re-engage, reimagine, and most importantly remind myself of who I was and why I came into the field to help.

CONCLUSION

In closing, it is essential for me to leverage these support systems to elevate my self-efficacy when encountering social constraints that suffocate my existence in an environment that historically was not intended for most of my identities. Routinely, our field stops short of carrying theory into practice on every level of interaction including to supporting the well-being of Black women. After all, Black women should not be relegated to shrink from their potential within an environment that consistently threatens their identities.

As a Black woman, I derive from an ancestral heritage of individuals who were not victims but victors over their circumstances. Therefore, I am not waiting for anyone to save me, but instead, I aspire to continue to be a change agent. Black women will continue to enter and excel in these environments that do not fully embrace their identities, but they should not have to confront racist, prejudice and discriminatory beliefs, practices, and policies in solitude.

REFERENCES

Bandura, A. (1997). *Self-efficacy: The exercise of control.* New York, NY: Freeman.

Burke, M. G., & Carter, J. D. (2015). Examining perceptions of networking among African American women in student affairs. *NASPA Journal About Women in Higher Education, 8*(2), 140–155.

Clifford, A. (2001). *Introducing feminist theology.* Maryknoll, NY: Orbis Books.

Evans, S. Y. (2008). *Black women in the ivory tower, 1850–1954: An Intellectual History.* Gainesville, FL: University Press of Florida.

Fiorenza, E. (1992). *In memory of her: A feminist theological construction of Christian origins.* New York, NY: Crossroads.

Hayden Glover, M. (2012). Existing pathways: A historical overview of Black women in higher education administration. In T. B. Jones, L. S. Dawkins, M. M. Mc-Clinton, & M. H. Glover (Eds.), *Pathways to higher education administration for African American women* (pp. 4–17). Sterling, VA: Stylus.

Higginbotham, E. (1997). The Black church: A gender perspective. In T. Fulop & A. Raboteau (Eds.), *African American religion: Interpretive essays in history and culture* (pp. 201–225). New York, NY: Routledge.

hooks, B. (2010). *Teaching critical thinking: Practical wisdom.* New York, NY: Routledge.

Howard-Hamilton, M. F. (2003). Theoretical frameworks for African American women. *New Directions for Student Services* (No. 104, pp. 19–27). San Francisco, CA: Jossey Bass.

Hughes, R. L., & Howard-Hamilton, M. F. (2003). Insights: Emphasizing issues that affect African American women. *New Directions for Student Services* (No. 104, pp. 95–104). San Francisco, CA: Jossey Bass.

Jones, C. P. (2000). Levels of racism: A theoretic framework and a gardener's tale. *American Journal of Public Health, 90*(8), 1212–1215.

Mattis, J. S. (2002). Religion and spirituality in the meaning–making and coping experiences of African American women: A qualitative analysis. *Psychology of Women Quarterly, 26*(4), 309–321.

McIntosh, P. (1988). *White privilege and male privilege: A personal account of coming to see correspondences through work in women's studies.* Wellesley, MA: Wellesley College, Center for Research on Women.

Mehra, A., Kilduff, M., & Brass, D. J. (1998). At the margins: A distinctiveness approach to the social identity and social networks of underrepresented groups. *Academy of Management Journal, 41*(4), 441–452.

Mitchell, D., Jr., & Westbrook, D. C. (2016). Developing multicultural competence for preparing student affairs professionals through a study away program. *Journal of College Student Development, 57*(8), 1056–1058.

Pajares, F. (1996). Self-efficacy beliefs in achievement settings. *Review of Educational Research, 66,* 543–578.

Patton, L. D., & Harper, S. R. (2003). Mentoring relationships among African American women in graduate and professional schools. *New Directions for Student Services* (No. 104, pp. 67–78). San Francisco, CA: Jossey-Bass.

Perkins, L. M. (1983). The impact of the "cult of true womanhood" on the education of Black women. *Journal of Social Issues, 39*(3), 17–28.

Pope, R. L., Mueller, J. A., & Reynolds, A. L. (2009). Looking back and moving forward: Future directions for diversity research in student affairs. *Journal of College Student Development, 50*(6), 640–658.

Pope, R. L., & Reynolds, A. L. (1997). Student affairs core competencies: Integrating multicultural awareness, knowledge, and skills. *Journal of College Student Development, 38*(3), 266–277.

Pope, R. L., Reynolds, A. L., & Mueller, J. A. (2014). *Creating multicultural change on campus.* San Francisco, CA: Jossey-Bass.

Solórzano, D., Ceja, M., & Yosso, T. (2000). Critical race theory, racial microaggressions, and campus racial climate: The experiences of African American college students. *Journal of Negro Education, 69*(1–2), 60–73.

Stewart, D. L. (2013). Racially minoritized students at U.S. four-year institutions. *The Journal of Negro Education, 82*(2), 184–197.

Vaughn-Hall, J. (2017, May 20). 13 *Angela Davis quotes that will make you proud to be a Black woman.* Retrieved May 6, 2018, from https://www.women.com/jasminevaughn/lists/number-angela-davis-quotes-that-will-make-you-proud-to-be-a-black-woman

Watt, S. K. (2013). Designing and implementing multicultural initiatives: Guiding principles. *New Directions for Student Services* (No. 144, pp. 5–15). San Francisco, CA: Jossey Bass.

CHAPTER 2

USING COUNTER-STORIES AS STRATEGIES TO NAVIGATE HOSTILE CAMPUS ENVIRONMENTS

Rodney Bates
University of Oklahoma

A large body of student affairs scholarship addresses barriers that students face in achieving their educational goals; however, the much literature does not examine challenges that student affairs professionals confront as they build their careers, especially those of color. This chapter will reflect on how I navigate microaggressions in a hostile campus culture as well as campus politics as a student affairs professional of color at a predominantly White institution (PWI). Through the technique of counter-storytelling, my experiences can shed light on some of the broader realities and circumstances facing people of color in the student affairs profession.

Student affairs professionals, according to James Rhatigan (2009), must continually educate themselves, conduct research, and produce scholarship concerning the profession that we hold dear. Addressing new and

No Ways Tired, pages 15–23
Copyright © 2019 by Information Age Publishing

traditional areas of student support, student affairs departments and professionals contribute to student learning and success as defined by students themselves and by other stakeholders within and beyond the boundaries of higher education (Schuh, Jones, & Harper, 2010). Student affairs departments exist to support students, build inclusive communities, and create learning environments outside the classroom. However, despite the plethora of multicultural centers, Greek life organizations, student leadership offices, and other student services on campuses across the country, many people of color and other marginalized student populations feel unwanted and unaccepted, as if they do not belong (Strayhorn, 2012). As higher education institutions create and promote personal growth and civil responsibility, they also need to assess campus climates, mission statements, values, and goals.

As a student affairs professional, I find that my experiences play a significant role in how I support students of color outside the classroom. Working in Residence Life gives me many opportunities to interact with people of color in non-academic settings. My professional journey started with a conversation that occurred during my first student affairs job. My colleague said to me, "I don't know why people of color are not successful at PWIs. Look at you; you made it." I was not sure how to respond to my colleague, but at the time, I had a tremendous amount of respect for him. I am sure his intentions were good, but I honestly did not feel that I had succeeded at my college, a PWI. I replied to him, "Define *succeed* or *being successful at a PWI.*" My colleague responds,

> Well, you know…what you are—educated. You have two degrees, a career, and you're a good citizen. I mean, the goal of the university is that you walk out of here with a degree and you have done that; so I would say that you have succeeded at making it. Plus, we have offices to assist students of color and the university has made the commitment for students to achieve. Hell! You have the multicultural office, student support services, and other areas in student affairs to give you all the assistance you need to make it if you want to.

I thought about the age-old claim that if someone really wants to make it, they can; which does not bother me as much as the assumption that if African Americans do fail, it's because they are lazy or did not try hard enough.

My colleague was convinced that he was right about African Americans' ability to succeed at PWIs because he knew from what and where I came. He was certain that the challenges I faced further supported the notion that African Americans can succeed at a PWI, but some simply choose not to. It is tough to have these kinds of conversations with people who have no clue about being disadvantaged. I knew that being silent would only make me a contributor to this ignorance, which is also burdensome. At the time, I did not understand as much as I do now, but this would be the beginning of my journey of being Black in student affairs.

In this chapter, I will explore my personal journey and reflect on how I navigate microaggressions (Smith, Hung, & Franklin, 2011), a hostile campus culture, and campus politics at a PWI as a student affairs professional of color. Through the technique of counter-storytelling, I hope my experiences will shed light on some of the broader realities and circumstances facing people of color in the student affairs profession.

THE JOURNEY

Educational research over the last few decades has documented the fact that the ivory tower is rife with systemic structural barriers that prevent students of color from attending, succeeding, and thriving at PWIs. Although most literature focuses mainly on students, academic and student affairs professionals of color face similar hurdles as well. Our challenges may differ from students' but are just as structurally unjust. As student affairs professionals, we often place others' needs before our own well-being. This reality is especially true for us as people of color. Many of us reflect on the person who took the time to invest in us and we try to do the same for the next generation. Thanks to the influential mentors in our own lives, we realize that one person or group can have a major influence on a young person's life and career path—in our case, steering us into the world of student affairs. We value the investment of time, effort, and love that these role models poured into us. These people changed our lives for the better—or so we think.

When I first entered the profession, I welcomed the opportunity to have a similar influence on students. I assumed that everyone else working in higher education, especially in student affairs, felt the same way. It did not occur to me that some colleagues and higher education employees had priorities different from mine and might not always place students' well-being at the center of their job. This realization occurred at the very beginning of my career.

Although I was steered toward student affairs work by my mentors, my career path actually was not straightforward. Immediately after completing my undergraduate degree in psychology, I went to work in the field of banking. I had planned to attend graduate school in industrial psychology, but the school I applied to turned out to be very competitive and I was denied admission. Therefore, banking would be my career path and I was glad to have a lucrative job, but I never felt fulfilled or satisfied. I continued reflecting on all the people at my university—people of color—who had poured into me while I was completing my degree. I said to myself, why am I not doing that? Twelve years later, I do not regret my decision to leave my well-paid bank job and to find employment in higher education. My motivation to help marginalized students had been a passion for me, even before I was aware of it, which would sustain and motivate me to seek my PhD.

WHAT ARE WE NAVIGATING?

As I simultaneously pursued my PhD and developed my student affairs career, I began to recognize and name the experiences I had as a Black person working in student affairs. I learned first-hand how White supremacy, hetero-patriarchy, and capitalist anti-Black structures are very much alive, active, and systemically operating in higher education. As a scholar, I use the following frameworks not only to navigate oppressive systems, but also to deconstruct, disrupt, and dismantle systems of oppression. This approach provides a pathway enabling professionals of color to focus on students who are marginalized by these systems.

Critical Race Theory

Critical race theory (CRT) draws from and extends a broad literature based in law, sociology, history, ethnic studies, education, and women's studies (Solórzano & Yosso, 2002a). CRT addresses the roles of race and racism in education including at the intersections of race, class, and gender (Solórzano & Yosso, 2002b). Using this framework, we can intentionally focus on the intersections of race, class, and gender while simultaneously addressing traditional paradigms such as classroom settings, administrative factors, institutional climate, and professional success measures.

Intersectionality

In her work on intersectionality, Crenshaw (1991) addressed how identities converge and how our experiences can be similar and different at the same time. Since Crenshaw's revolutionary contribution to intersectionality, scholars have asserted that individuals have many identities and that focusing on only one identity leads to a failure to understand how the person's multiple identities interact in ways that affect their experiences. Understanding how these multiple identities intersect provides a more holistic understanding of individuals and their experiences.

Using intersectionality provides a framework that analyzes on a micro level, the intersections of multiple identities and on a macro level, the structural and political systems. Structural intersectionality refers to how multiple social systems interact to shape individuals' experiences, especially their experiences of oppression (Crenshaw, 1991). In higher education, an example of structural intersectionality is the shaping of Black male's experiences at PWIs through the combination of sexual orientation and racial inequalities. Political intersectionality refers to "how the multiple social groups to which an individual belongs pursue different political agendas, which can function to silence the voices of those who are at the intersection of those social groups" (Museus & Griffin, 2011, p. 7). For example, political intersectionality is at play when Black males refuse to address discrimination against lesbian, gay, bisexual, and transgender (LGBT) students of color to avoid having these issues made public and "risking tainting the image of those communities of color" (Museus & Griffin, 2011, p. 7).

Counter-Storytelling

The aforementioned concepts lead me to my last conceptual framework and, most importantly, to ways to disrupt the system of oppression. Counter-storytelling is an essential method of CRT (Matsuda, 1991). Counter-story-telling not only gives voice to people of color, but also serves as a way to disrupt the dominant discourses (Hunn, Guy, & Manglitz, 2006). Solórzano and Yosso (2002b) define counter-storytelling as "a method of telling the stories of those people whose experiences are not often told" (p. 26). *Personal stories or narratives* "recount an individual's experiences with various forms of racism and sexism" (Solórzano & Yosso, 2002b, p. 32). Additionally, I draw from critical race scholars Dr. Theodorea Regina Berry and Dr. David O. Stovall in using *hope narratives* to honor what should be a reality and not just a hope (Berry & Stovall, 2013).

WHAT DID I JUST HEAR?

I was at a conference in Chicago with a few of my White colleagues and we all decided to grab some famous GiGi's pizza. This conference was not our first attending together, so I felt relatively safe attending with my colleagues (I thought). We all ate and had a great time. We began to bundle up and head for the exit as we decided to walk around for a bit, maybe find a club or bar. As we were walking, we noticed we were a bit lost and soon were in an unfamiliar area. I was aware of all the negative talk in the media about violence in Chicago, but in my mind, I never felt we were in danger. Some of my colleagues, though, not only took Chicago's reputation at face value but even started making negative comments about the city, completely disregarding its historical context. I was not as knowledgeable then as I am now, but I was aware that there were larger issues at play in Chicago beyond the media's narrative of violence. As we walked, a few of my colleagues expressed fear, and that's their right—we could debate why some other time. I figured out where we were, which was just down the street from locations that were familiar to us. Despite all the jokes, I felt confident and said, "Hey you all, it's all good, I think we will be okay." I remember my White male colleague turning to me and saying in front of everybody, "Hey, you're not Black enough." He proceeded to go in a different direction and told the group to follow him. I was shocked, angry, paralyzed, and in pure rage at the comment; not because they didn't follow me, but because my identity was questioned and disregarded. My other colleagues laughed as if it was just some simple joke and walked in his direction. This insult provoked an emotional and physiological response stronger than any other that I can remember. After I gathered myself together, I caught up with the group. I just remember being silent, angry, and discouraged. I still had to go back and work with this individual and did not really know how to work with him as a team player after he made that comment.

Similar stories happen all the time for professionals of color in higher education. When faced with such experiences, how do you navigate actions that devalue you as a human being? What do you say when your colleagues ask why you don't smile? What do you do when they ask you about all the students of color, as if you were the designated spokesperson for all things Black, all things racial, and all things lower-income? Similarly, when they treat you as if you were a Google search engine when they seek any kind of information about "diversity?" What do you think when they pass you up for promotion after promotion? How do you respond when they are passive-aggressive in person but throw you under the bus in email? What do you do when they refuse to acknowledge an unequal playing field? How do you react when their nuances of ostensibly meritocratic language treat you as exotic or over-sensationalize you or when they export your labor as a favor they are doing for you? When they unconsciously and consciously refuse to acknowledge your identities except in negative and dehumanizing ways? When they display white tears for no reason, "averted gazes, exasperated looks" (Delgado & Stefancic, 1997)? When they use code words like "quotas" and "affirmative action" and comments such as "You're not like the rest of them" and "I don't think of you as Black" (Solórzano, 1998)? When they refuse to believe your story, narrative, situation, or perspective? When your colleague maintains complete silence in times of unjust policies, programs, and ideologies? When they question why you hired so many people of color, but get angry when you ask why they did not hire a single person of color? Why do they claim to be an ally, but never speak up publicly? When you endure all this and so many more macro and micro aggressions, how do you not get tired and give up?

RECOMMENDATIONS

There is no single solution that fits every situation. Successfully navigating as a person of color in student affairs certainly depends on the institutional climate, politics, resources, and support available. However, I can share the strategies that have worked for me as a professional.

- *Invest in a community of support that reflects your racial, ethnic, or cultural identity.* In doing so, you provide yourself a base of support to refuel and to be heard.
- *Incorporate self-care as professional development.* Communicate with your supervisor or employer that self-care allows you to be aware of your physical, mental, and spiritual well-being, which makes you more effective in your work with students and colleagues.
- *Collaborate with colleagues from across campus.* Too often, we remain isolated in our own departmental or disciplinary bubble, but we cannot assume that everyone knows the work we do. Cross-departmental collaboration is particularly effective with campus entities that engage intentionally in social justice as part of their core mission, and this can give you some institutional agency beyond student affairs.
- *Be reflective but also intersectional.* Being reflective allows you to analyze the areas where you excel as well as those where you have room to grow. This process shows us that we also occupy some spaces of privilege. Acknowledging these hidden privileges while occupying marginalizing spaces can prevent us from reproducing or reinforcing oppressive systems (Crenshaw, 1989).
- *Seek counseling if needed.* Mental health care has long been stigmatized, but racial trauma can be passed down through the generations (Carter, 2007). It just makes sense to seek professional counseling to deal with the many facets of our society's insidious racism. In doing so, you can acquire the proper processing and healthier coping mechanisms.

While I hope these strategies will be helpful and relevant to people of color working in student affairs, I truly believe that those who benefit the most work in systems that put forth the most effort to facilitate a supportive work environment that fosters success for professionals of color. I also draw from Leigh Patel's *Decolonizing Educational Research: From Ownership to Answerability* (2015). We will no longer need special strategies for navigating as a student affairs professional of color when those in power critically and intentionally divest themselves of their Whiteness and dismantle the oppressive hetero-patriarchal capitalist values of White supremacy (Patel, 2015). Until then, take care . . . self-care.

HOPE NARRATIVE

I was at a conference in Chicago with a few of my White colleagues and we all decided to grab some famous GiGi's pizza. This was not our first conference together, so I felt relatively safe attending with my colleagues (I thought). We all ate and had a great time. We began to bundle up and head for the exit as we decided to walk around for a bit, maybe find a club or bar. As we were walking, we noticed we were a bit lost. I felt confident and said, "Hey you all, it's all good, I think we will be okay." My White colleagues remained supportive and silent. We reached our destination.

REFERENCES

Berry, T. R., & Stovall, D. O. (2013). Trayvon Martin and the curriculum of tragedy: Critical race lessons for education. *Race Ethnicity and Education, 16*(4), 587–602.

Carter, R. T. (2007). Racism and psychological and emotional injury: Recognizing and assessing race-based traumatic stress. *The Counseling Psychologist, 35*(1), 13–105.

Crenshaw, K. (1989). Demarginalizing the intersection of race and sex: A Black feminist critique of antidiscrimination doctrine, feminist theory and antiracist politics. *University of Chicago Legal Forum, 1*(8), 139–167. Retrieved from http://chicagounbound.uchicago.edu/uclf/vol1989/iss1/8

Crenshaw, K. (1991). Mapping the margins: Intersectionality, identity politics, and violence against women of color. *Stanford Law Review, 43*(6), 1241–1299.

Delgado, R., & Stefancic, J. (1997). (Eds.). *Critical White studies: Looking behind the mirror*. Philadelphia, PA: Temple University Press.

Hunn, L., Guy, T., & Manglitz, E. (2006). *Who can speak for whom? Using counter-story-telling to challenge racial hegemony*. Adult Education Research Conference, University of Minnesota, Minneapolis, MN. Retrieved from https://newprairiepress.org/cgi/viewcontent.cgi?referer=https://us.search.yahoo.com/&httpsredir=1&article=2503&context=aerc

Matsuda, C. (1991). Voices of America: Accent, anti-discrimination law, and a jurisprudence for the last reconstruction. *Yale Law Journal, 100*, 1329–1407.

Museus, S. D., & Griffin, K. A. (2011). Mapping the margins in higher education: On the promise of intersectionality frameworks in research and discourse. *New Directions for Institutional Research, 2011*(151), 5–13.

Patel, L. (2015). *Decolonizing educational research: From ownership to answerability*. New York, NY: Routledge.

Rhatigan, J. J. (2009). A brief history of student affairs administration. In J. H. Schuh, S. R. Jones, & S. R. Harper (Eds.), *Student services: A handbook for the profession*. (pp. 3-18). San Francisco, CA: Wiley.

Schuh, J. H., Jones, S. R., & Harper, S. R. (2010). *Student services: A handbook for the profession*. San Francisco, CA: Wiley.

Smith, W. A., Hung, M., & Franklin, J. D. (2011). Racial battle fatigue and the miseducation of Black men: Racial microaggressions, societal problems, and environmental stress. *The Journal of Negro Education, 80*(1), 63–82.

Solorzano, D. G., & Yosso, T. J. (2002a). A critical race counterstory of race, racism, and affirmative action. *Equity & Excellence in Education, 35*(2), 155–168.

Solórzano, D. G., & Yosso, T. J. (2002b). Critical race methodology: Counter-storytelling as an analytical framework for education research. *Qualitative Inquiry, 8*(1), 23–44.

Strayhorn, T. L. (2012). *College students' sense of belonging: A key to educational success for all students.* New York, NY: Routledge.

CHAPTER 3

RISING ABOVE INTERNALIZED OPPRESSION

Strategies to Thrive as a Professional of Color

Araceli Cruz
Linfield College

As a first-generation, mid-level, Latina professional, I have found four strategies that help me thrive in my career trajectory in higher education: mentoring, professional development, self-care within community, and staff–student relationships. These tenets construct my vision for institutional environments that are inclusive of professionals of color. This chapter provides strategies to combat internalized oppression and imposter syndrome as a professional of color in higher education institutions.

My career in higher education is the through the lens of the financial aid field, which is often overlooked for the critical role it plays in supporting student success. Serving as a financial aid administrator at predominantly White institutions has felt isolating and exhausting on multiple occasions throughout my professional career. The financial aid system is full of federal

No Ways Tired, pages 25–33
Copyright © 2019 by Information Age Publishing

regulations and procedures with very little space for equity work within the broader system. Although Financial Aid can be very transactional, I always approach my work from a social justice lens. In order for me to stay true to my mission of serving underrepresented students, my work as a college administrator expands beyond my office walls. Despite the daily challenges in higher education, my community continually reminds me of how important my work is. This collective ideology helps me remain aware of the constant struggle that still exists in our communities of color and gives purpose to what can often be transactional work.

As a first-generation, mid-level, and Latina professional, I found four strategies that have helped me thrive during my career trajectory in higher education: mentoring, professional development, self-care within community, and student relationships. These tenets constructed my vision for institutional environments that are inclusive of individuals of color. They helped me combat the impostor syndrome, and fear of speaking up when I was the only person of color in the room, when my projects failed, or when I felt overwhelmed.

In my first years in higher education, I was eagerly creating a strong base of individuals to support me in my work that was vital to my career to help me. I wanted my work to change lives. As a young staff member of color, I found that trajectory. These people validated me, invested in me, challenged me, and helped me grow. As I moved through different stages in my life, my support group naturally expanded with individuals from all walks of life.

MENTORING

While the concept of mentoring is not new, the definition has evolved. As adapted from Luedke (2017), mentoring refers to a mutually beneficial relationship built on trust between an advanced career incumbent (mentor) and a beginner (mentee) aimed at promoting career growth for both. Torres and Hernandez (2009) describe the various roles mentors play in the development of their mentees. Those roles include, but are not limited to, enhancing the skills and intellectual development of a mentee; having a sponsor to facilitate a mentee's entry and advancement; helping the mentee understand organizational values, culture, customs, resources, and key players; and acting as a source of support (see also Luedke, 2017). These mentoring capacities further define the role that a mentor plays in the career trajectory of their mentee. Mentoring requires support, encouragement, and coaching, not just networking opportunities (Torres & Hernandez, 2009).

The most common mentoring relationships tend to occur between members of the same race and gender, which allows individuals to share cultural sensitivities and discover similarities. However, some institutions still do not have many staff members of color (Turner, 2002). While institutions have been intentional in hiring more student affairs professionals of color, high-level administration positions are still held predominantly by White males (Torres & Hernandez, 2009). The lack of proper representation in high-level executive leadership often creates barriers for the staff of color to build same race and gender mentoring relationships. In my experience thus far, finding mentors from my own race was easier than finding female mentors. While I found all my mentoring relationships to be critical and necessary for my personal and career growth, it is important to note that there were significant challenges to cross-gender mentoring relationships. One major challenge was around the gender-based power imbalances these types of mentoring relationships created. However, intentional cross-gender mentoring relationships can have a positive impact on women of color. These types of relationships aid women of color to overcome barriers to socialization in the workplace (Aguirre, 2000). In general, studies show that those who experience supportive relationships such as mentoring have more opportunities for success, advancement, and achievement in their careers (Ruth, 2012). Building authentic connections through mentoring relationships advances equity work by improving staff retention and campus climate. As the growing body of literature on mentoring indicates, a person's career can be significantly impacted by having a mentor (Salazar, 2009).

During my first job in higher education, my supervisor was a Latino male who was highly respected both in the financial aid field and the Latino-American community. He informally became one of my mentors along my career path as I developed into a financial aid administrator. While I am not suggesting that all supervisors become mentors, it is possible that mentors can be supervisors. Having a supervisor who was a person of color (specifically, who belonged to my racial group) provided me with a safe space to flourish into who I am today.

One afternoon, I walked into his office to talk about the concept of saying no without feeling guilty. We discussed how growing up as a Latina woman, it was unacceptable to question authority, especially male authority. Following this conversation, my mentor took steps to help me elevate my voice in the workplace. He intentionally sought my feedback on current or new office policies and encouraged me to lead staff meetings. He coached me on how to advocate for myself and my students. Most importantly, he created a safe space for me to disagree with him constructively. I learned to push myself out of my comfort zone, take risks, and find my voice as a Latina professional. I always felt equal to him and valued for the contributions I brought to the office. Although my supervisor was aware of his privilege and the power dynamics that influenced our mentor–mentee relationship, up until this point, I was the only one benefiting from this relationship. I struggled for quite some time with the narrow role I played as a mentee.

However, as I matured in my mentoring relationships, I realized that he was also going through his own career journey. Mentoring is essential for student affairs administrators of color, both as a vital tenet of our career development and as a necessary tool for survival in institutions of higher education. Likewise, as a mentee of color, it is crucial to understand the role individuals play in furthering and supporting leaders of color.

PROFESSIONAL DEVELOPMENT

Professional development, as described by Schwartz and Bryan (1998), refers to the various types of educational experiences and ongoing training related to an individual's work. These opportunities aim to enhance the competencies, skills, and knowledge of individuals, and enable them to provide better services to their constituents (Schwartz & Bryan, 1998).

When support or mentors of color are not available within a department or even at the institution, professional development can be a practical tool for receiving the necessary support to be successful in one's career. Seeking and engaging in various types of professional progression is transformative because it allows an individual to grow both as a person and as a professional (Schwartz & Bryan, 1998). Getting involved on campus in different capacities allows staff members of color to gain a better understanding of the institutional climate and connect with like-minded colleagues. Institutions often have ways for staff to participate in search committees, campus-wide meetings, and teach-in luncheons, among other ways to contribute.

Being actively involved outside of one's campus can also provide valuable learning experiences. Off-campus trainings through outside organizations provide staff with insight on various leadership styles, as well as various programs offered throughout higher education (Gardner & Barnes, 2007). Furthermore, engaging in off-campus events is another way to develop new friendships and connect with other individuals who hold similar values or positions that you may be interested in exploring at some point in your career trajectory.

Thomas and Hollenshead (2002) state that staff of color are overtaxed with requests to serve in various capacities beyond their full-time job, which resonates with me as the financial aid field in Oregon lacks racial and economic diversity. When I began my first job, I was excited to attend every training, conference, and campus committee to which I was invited. Being a bilingual and bicultural Latina in a state with very few administrators of color gave me a lot of exposure to opportunities. I quickly realized that being involved in too many committees or being away from my office often created time management challenges. I was feeling burnt out as I consistently found myself trying to catch up with work. I was staying later at the office, regularly checking my emails after hours, and began working on the weekends. The concept of a work–life balance vanished. As I tried to balance my professional development and workload, I realized that I had a responsibility to be accessible to Latinx students and their families. I came to understand that not having a work–life balance not only impacted my own sense of stability, but was also affecting my ability to serve my students.

I learned that career development came with the responsibility of intentionality and authentic self-assessment. As it related to financial aid, I was confident in knowing my strengths as well as what gaps existed in my skills. I became more intentional about seeking opportunities that challenged me and helped me to become a better-rounded administrator.

I found that resources allocated for development vary from one institution to the next. Often, departments will have budgets that limit the number of times you can attend off-campus trainings or conferences. I took ownership of my career trajectory by incorporating professional development into my personal budget. I found ways to make trainings more affordable (e.g., presenting at conferences for discounted registration fees, partnering with my peers to share lodging costs, and taking advantage of webinars). It is essential for people of color to find intentional ways to invest in themselves, especially when the institution is unwilling or unable to do so (Thomas & Hollenshead, 2002).

Professional development is a tool that has helped me to thrive as a staff of color in higher education. The tools and knowledge I gain by investing in myself serve as a way of dismantling my own internalized oppression and quiets down the inner thoughts of self-doubt. As I mature in my career, I have to practice balancing my own needs and the needs of my community which I work passionately to serve. In order to be a successful and effective agent of change I must lead with intentionality and purpose.

SELF-CARE WITHIN COMMUNITY

My career as a financial aid administrator of color has served as a vehicle to fulfill my life purpose of serving underrepresented students in higher education. As I continue to grow and develop as a leader, I gain clarity on how structural inequalities and institutional racism negatively impact how staff of color advance social justice and equity work at their institutions.

A growing body of research highlights how institutional racism still impacts historically marginalized groups, including faculty of color at predominantly White institutions. Repeated studies have further illustrated that while faculty of color may experience fulfillment from different aspects of their careers, feelings of isolation, marginalization, frustration, hurt, and anger are also at the forefront of their experiences (Salazar, 2009). The themes of marginalization found with faculty of color seem to resonate for those in non-faculty roles (Salazar, 2009) though there is limited research on the experiences of administrators and staff of color at predominantly White institutions. While being an individual of color means enduring intentional and unintentional systemic racism, it can be challenging and demoralizing at times. hooks (1989) contributed to this state of marginality, asserting it is "much more than a site of deprivation, it is also a site of radical possibility, a space of resistance" (p. 20). To continue being fulfilled by the work we have chosen to do, it is important to take care of ourselves by finding spaces of resistance. hooks states that spaces where one can share stories of oppression in a community of resistance are critical for higher educational professionals, because "without such spaces, we would not survive" (p. 19). For people of color "who are unwilling to play the roles of "exotic other," [we] must create spaces within that culture of domination ... to survive whole, [with] our souls intact" (p. 19). Witnessing and enduring systemic racism can be challenging, and therefore, we must be better at using the system to our advantage. hooks continues to elaborate on the distinction between marginality imposed on us by oppressive structures versus the marginality one chooses as a status of resistance. Choosing marginalization as a state of resistance allows an individual to work through personal struggle and pain and is also an opportunity to heal as a community collectively. It can be a challenge for individuals to remember their purpose if feelings of isolation and the imposter syndrome, fear of being discovered as a fraud, are present (Gardner & Holley, 2011).

When I started my role in higher education, I experienced what many professionals of color experience when they try to take on systemic oppression. I quickly found that the changes I wanted to implement were rejected by leaders who were not ready to take on the heavy lifting. These experiences left me feeling disappointed and angry. During the first year on the job, I was selected to join a leadership program along with various Latinx leaders from all over the state. The goal of this statewide leadership program was to strengthen networks across sectors to move our community's Latinx agenda forward cohesively while developing skills to heal from internalized oppression and its effects (Luna Jiménez, 2012). This group provided a brave space to address past hurts that were getting in the way of supporting others authentically. Most importantly, it was a space in which I could separate myself from the institutional oppression I consumed every day. Processing my feelings allowed me to validate myself and continue to find ways to interrupt systemic oppression for my community. I find that staying connected to the community, more specifically my networks, prevents me from feeling isolated and helps me to continue advocating for important change.

One of the most effective ways for me to battle feelings of marginalization or imposter syndrome is taking care of myself through my community. Gaining distance from negative experiences while in the company of my community allows me to regain energy and purpose. Community for me means being with people or in spaces, which can counteract my internalized oppression, validate my existence as a Latina woman, and share similar social justice values. I have built a diverse network of family, friends, and colleagues who understand and validate the experiences we have as people of color. These "spaces of resistance," as referred to by hooks (2014), help me to regain hope, love, creativity, and validation of my existence as a human being.

STAFF–STUDENT RELATIONSHIPS

It is important to me that my students' experiences are heard and validated regardless of their race or gender. For students of color, validation is especially critical for their successful navigation in higher education. Rendon's (1994) validation theory supports this practice and defines validation as "an enabling, confirming and the supportive process initiated by in-and-out-of-class agents that fosters academic and interpersonal development" (p. 44). Although providing students validation for their experiences may seem like an easy task, studies reveal that White staff and administrators historically did not holistically support students of color. Instead, they focused on students' academic experiences and neglected other factors that affected their time in college, such as personal or familial concerns (Luedke, 2017). Furthermore, a growing body of research adds that students of color seek relationships with professionals of color because they address students' lives inside and outside of the academy. Therefore, students of color seek to develop more holistic and authentic relationships with staff of color (Luedke, 2017).

Yosso's (2005) six forms of community cultural wealth capitals—aspirational, familial, social, linguistic, navigational, and resistant capital—provide an asset-based framework for staff to better support students from underrepresented communities. As a first-generation college student, authentic relationships were the reason I survived college. I struggled during my first year in college until I met two Latina professors who helped me gain the social capital (social connections) and the cultural capital (skills and knowledge) needed to succeed (Yosso, 2005). My professors intentionally and mindfully nurtured my cultural strengths in an environment operating under a deficit model. While I have not served as a faculty member, I have viewed my role to be similar in how I support students.

One day, I received an email from a faculty member who was very concerned about one of their students. However, the concern was not about financial aid, but instead about the student's mental health. The student identified as Latinx and disclosed having difficulty connecting with others on campus. The student was eager to connect with me and set up an appointment immediately following the introduction email made by their professor. During our meeting, this student disclosed that they felt depressed, had difficulty leaving their room, and were falling behind in classes. I guided the conversation to see if they could identify what was triggering those feelings of distress. It did not take long before they broke into tears and shared with me that their mother was struggling with food insecurities. They confessed that they were thinking of withdrawing because it was difficult to concentrate while thinking about their family on top of feeling out of place at the school. I took the liberty of sharing parts of my undergraduate experience that was like theirs. We spent much of our time together brainstorming ways they could stay connected with their family while also focusing on school. At the end of the meeting, they hugged me and said, "I am so happy I got connected to you. It is like you get me. You really get all of me."

I checked back in with this student towards the latter part of the semester. They shared that after our conversation, they went home and set their mom up with food resources. They earned A's and B's on their midterms and were happy to let me know they would be staying at the school. They successfully graduated as the first person in their family to receive a bachelor's degree. My lived experience as a first-generation Latina college student helped me support and validate this student. Stories like these help me remember that the only way to effectively dismantle institutional oppression is one student at a time.

CONCLUSION

Student affairs professionals of color are an essential part of the higher education community. At the same time, staff of color continue to face a myriad of challenges related to the structural racism that exists at predominantly White institutions. Although it is critical to understand how these systems impact both administrators and students of color, it is equally important to understand the power one has to continue perpetuating or interrupting institutional oppression. While my educational and vocational experience has been limited to predominantly White, private institutions, I center my narrative on how I continue to find ways to not only survive but to thrive, carrying out social justice and equity work. The strategies I recommend in this chapter continue to remind me of my purpose in higher education and provide me with a framework for understanding how I can rise above systemic structures that have marginalized me as a woman of color.

Without mentoring, professional development, staff–student relationships, and self-care within a community, I would be paralyzed by my internalized oppression and the reality of the work I do. Financial aid is transactional by default, but when I work with underrepresented students, I know first-hand what it means to be in their seat. Removing financial barriers for low-income students of color gives me energy to speak up even when I am the only person of color in the room.

REFERENCES

Aguirre, A., Jr. (2000). *Women and minority faculty in the academic workplace: Recruitment, retention, and academic culture.* ASHE-ERIC Higher Education Report, *27*(6). San Francisco, CA: Jossey-Bass.

Gardner, S. K., & Barnes, B. J. (2007). Graduate student involvement: Socialization for the professional role. *Journal of College Student Development, 48*(4), 369–387.

Gardner, S. K., & Holley, K. A. (2011). "Those invisible barriers are real": The progression of first-generation students through doctoral education. *Equity & Excellence in Education, 44*(1), 77–92.

hooks, b. (1989). Choosing the margin as a space of radical openness. *Framework: The Journal of Cinema and Media, 36,* 15–23.

Luedke, C. L. (2017). Person first, student second: Staff and administrators of color supporting students of color authentically in higher education. *Journal of College Student Development, 58*(1), 37–52.

Luna Jiménez, N. (2012, June 8). *Transformational communication alliance building and authentic Latin@ leadership* [PDF]. Seminar presented at the Unid@s Cohort Retreat, Eugene, OR.

Rendon, L. I. (1994). Validating culturally diverse students: Toward a new model of learning and student development. *Innovative Higher Education, 19*(1), 33–51.

Ruth, S. (2012). *Leadership and liberation: A psychological approach.* New York, NY: Routledge.

Salazar, C. F. (2009). Strategies to survive and thrive in academia: The collective voices of counseling faculty of color. *International Journal for the Advancement of Counselling, 31*(3), 181–198.

Schwartz, R. A., & Bryan, W. A. (1998). What is professional development? *New Directions for Student Services, 1998*(84), 3–13.

Thomas, G. D., & Hollenshead, C. (2001). Resisting from the margins: The coping strategies of Black women and other women of color faculty members at a research university. *Journal of Negro Education, 70*(3), 166–175.

Torres, V., & Hernandez, E. (2009). Influence of an identified advisor/mentor on urban Latino students' college experience. *Journal of College Student Retention: Research, Theory & Practice, 11*(1), 141–160.

Turner, C. S. V. (2002). Women of color in academe: Living with multiple marginality. *The Journal of Higher Education, 73*(1), 74–93.

Yosso, T. J. (2005). Whose culture has capital? A critical race theory discussion of community cultural wealth. *Race Ethnicity and Education, 8*(1), 69–91.

CHAPTER 4

MÍ LATINA FEMINIST VOZ

Time for Conversation

Rocío Durán Hernández
Ventura College

I entered the field of student affairs naïve to the microaggressions I would experience based on my gender, ethnicity, and age. I was empowered by my own experiences, through my education and passion for social justice to pursue a career within higher education. It did not take me long to experience gender and race-based discrimination. The political environment has propelled me to question the lack of conversations about our experiences as women of color within student affairs. We need to bring awareness to the continued issues and find solutions to support women of color within the profession.

Through my personal experiences over the years, I continue to be on the receiving end of stereotypes for being a Latina woman. I have been subjected to unrealistic standards imposed on women and not necessarily men. As I learn about the experiences of some of my female colleagues, I conclude that we do not talk enough about the issues of perceptions and stereotypes towards women of color in the profession; there continues to be a lack of awareness. There are underlying assumptions that continue to impact

No Ways Tired, pages 35–41
Copyright © 2019 by Information Age Publishing

women of color and prevent us from excelling in the profession. There is more we can do in the realm of conversations and mentorship to combat the stereotypes and support women of color in student affairs.

GENDER EXPECTATIONS

In an assessment of the current state of women student affairs administrators, Yakaboski and Donaboo (2011) found that women of color continue to face obstacles in relation to race, class, and gender in higher education. There are continued social assumptions that men and women are different and are expected to perform within their gender roles. These social assumptions impact women in the workplace, often relegated to roles that rely on emotions and nurturing. In a study that compared the ratings of a successful middle manager of a man and a woman in the managing profession, Sümer (2006) found that the women were rated the lowest in task orientation and emotional stability. The study found that the middle manager position was gender-typed in favor of men, showing that gender-based assumptions impact women's opportunities in middle management. As Yakaboski and Donahoo (2011) point out, "The position occupied by student affairs and student service departments within higher education exemplifies both the assumptions about separate spheres and the gendered structure of the workplace" (p. 280). The organizational culture can also have a greater impact on the career choices that women make (Yakaboski & Donaboo, 2011).

In thinking about my own experiences, situations where gender-based assumptions existed had an impact on my own work. I recall a moment when I was yelled at inside my own office by an older male colleague. Aside from sharing the incident with my supervisor at the time, no type of action was taken to prevent the incident from reoccurring. This lack of action became a stressor in the workplace that eventually led me to leave that particular workplace environment. As noted by Gorena (1996),

> ...successful women in leadership positions must engage in gender-stereo-typed team play activities...This implies that women seeking advancement must adapt to rules established by men in power or be willing to engage in similar activities. However, the literature also reveals that women pursuing advancement, who assume characteristics attributed to males in similar situations, also run the risk of being perceived negatively by their peers. (p. 3)

I was reminded of incidents like these as I read about Hillary Rodham Clinton's own experiences as the first female democratic presidential candidate. As Rodham Clinton (2017) described, "It gets worse the higher you rise" (p. 119). There is a double standard that Rodham Clinton experienced during the election that I believe exists in the workplace. If I had yelled at this male colleague in his office, I wonder if, as in Sümer's (2006) study, I would have been rated low in emotional stability. We need to speak of these experiences to help us reflect on how we will move forward to remove these gender-based stereotypes from continuing to impact women's career trajectories (Yakaboski & Donahoo, 2011).

It does not escape me that Rodham Clinton is a White woman in politics and in the public eye. Nonetheless, her experiences as a woman, in general, are relatable. As a Latina professional, my experiences within the field of student affairs have been impacted by my ethnic background and gender. In a research study focused on women of color in academe, Sotello Viernes Turner (2002) discusses the concept of being "defined out" (p. 74). As women of color, we face multiple marginalities and often do not fit in or are left out of both the experiences of people of color and of women (Sotello Viernes Turner, 2002). In another study of career satisfaction and sex discrimination, Blackhurst (2000) found that women of color experience more sex discrimination than White women. This study, however, lacked representation with only 50 out of 307 participants being women of color, and only six of these participants being Hispanic (Blackhurst, 2000).

Although I have had support from people throughout my education and my career, I cannot help but feel that we do not talk enough about our experiences as women of color. I learned to be a strong woman from my mother as I saw her make her best attempt at balancing work inside and outside of the home. She was my first example of a working woman. These observations helped shape my own work ethic and develop perseverance. If anything has truly helped me thrive in the profession, it has been the example of my own Mexican mother.

CULTURAL EXPECTATIONS

Being born into a Mexican family, I was raised with familial standards that do not necessarily fit American society. As Moraga and Anzaldúa (2015) write, "The woman of color life is the crossroad, where no aspect of our identity is wholly dismissed from our consciousness..." (p. xxii). Outside of work, I experience the constant pressure of my culture's traditional norms and that of American society. In my culture, the expectation is not only to get married, but to have children. These societal expectations are so ingrained that we often ask these questions of each other as colleagues within the profession. Gender expectations of having a family, more often than not, add personal stress that can impact women's careers (Howard-Hamilton & Williams, 1996).

In her book about the 2016 presidential election, Rodham Clinton (2017) wrote about how challenging it is for women to be in politics. I contend her perception applies to education, and likely, the majority of professions. Rodham Clinton (2017) wrote,

> If we're too soft, we're not cut out for the big leagues. If we work too hard, we're neglecting our families. If we put family first, we're not serious about the work. If we have a career but no children, there's something wrong with us, and vice versa. (p. 119)

I grew up in community where we often celebrated religious events and holidays within our housing complex. Everyone involved contributed to the celebrations collectively. Being individualistic, as is the expectation in American society, has been challenging for me. I think of others first before I think of myself; however, as noted by Harris Canul (2003), collectivism is a value that can be beneficial in a team setting. Seeking advancement is also individualistic and self-promoting. As a Latina, self-promotion does not come easy; it means putting myself before others, something that is culturally not the norm. As Harris Canul (2003) writes, "It is a difficult balancing act to both be true to my culture by maintaining a sense of modesty in the workplace, and at the same time to publicly take ownership for my accomplishments" (p. 179). Understanding the cultural differences can help create a more supportive environment for women of color. In agreement with Harris Canul (2003), I expect my supervisors and colleagues to notice my hard work without having to self-promote my own accomplishments.

"YOUNG"

I recently participated in a panel for graduate students in a college counseling program where I described some of my own experiences in the profession. I shared that I am often judged for being "too young" and underestimated for being a woman. I often experience microaggressions related to my age. I have been hearing the "you're still young" phrase since I was in my graduate program for my master's degree. Several of the female students approached me after the panel sharing similar feelings. The issue of sex discrimination in student affairs is not new and women of color who perceive sex discrimination often experience career dissatisfaction (Blackhurst, 2000). I am certain a significant number of women within the profession have their own testimonies on this subject matter. In the end, I become frustrated when I feel others placing limitations on my abilities because of their own stereotypes.

RECOGNIZING INJUSTICE

To understand how I survive and continue to thrive in my career, I cannot help but think back to how I grew up. As a young Latina, I was encouraged to get an education and go to college by my parents. I grew up observing a lot as a young child and I have memories of moments that shape the way I see the world. I observed my mother getting turned away from services because the person behind the counter claimed to not speak our language. Accordingly, "My politics as a woman are deeply rooted in my immigrant parents' and my own past" (Yamada, 2015, p. 71). My observations and experiences from a young age gave me a reason to pursue an education and I am a first-generation college graduate. Furthermore, I identify as a Latina feminist as my culture and my gender, intertwined with my education, have influenced my perspectives in ways I could not have expected.

GUILT TRIP

My experiences did not come without guilt. I felt guilt about being away from home, getting a college education, and not knowing how to explain to my family what kind of job a degree with a double major in Chicana/o studies and Spanish would get me. As I moved on to my master's degree program, I felt even more guilt. I was removing myself from my goal of beginning to work full time immediately after earning my bachelor's degree. Internally, I felt obligated to give back to my parents and help financially. As Covarrubias, Romero, and Trivelli (2014) state, "... first-generation college students and Mexican descent students may feel that their individual academic achievements may disrupt the harmony of existing family relationships that are based on collective family needs and obligations" (p. 2032). Guilt also comes from not being physically present at home (Covarrubias et al., 2014).

It was during my time as a graduate student in my counseling program that I realized how much guilt I was carrying on my shoulders. Not surprisingly, guilt is a common symptom in the mental health of first generation college students (Covarrubias et al., 2014). Through my education, I was participating in an individualistic society and, at the same time, I was trying to maintain connection to my roots. As Moraga (2015) describes, "I am a woman with a foot in both worlds; and I refuse the split" (p. 29). My strategy became aligning myself with my classmates and finding the commonalities that brought us to our career. Members of my graduate program cohort became another familial presence for me.

MENTORSHIP

I navigated my career in student affairs by learning from folks within the profession who are more experienced and knowledgeable than I am. The mentorship I have received from colleagues within student affairs has been instrumental to my career decisions. I aspire to find that Latina who is in the higher-ranking leadership role that I desire, one to whom I could relate and talk to about not just women issues, but cultural issues. As noted by Dunbar and Kinnersley (2011), mentoring is important for women who aspire administrative roles and they suggest that institutions of higher education should promote a mentorship culture. In my own quest, I found a limited number of Latina women in the leadership roles I aspire to be in. Like Harris Canul (2003), "I also did not realize that having a hard-earned doctorate from a reputable institution still would not be enough for a Latina to be considered a true professional" (p. 167). As I have gone on through my career, I found my network of people who I can reach out to for guidance, mentorship, support, or simply a listening ear. The gender, roles, age, and aspirations of these folks vary.

CONCLUSION

As I continue to grow in my career, I have become more comfortable with owning my values and staying true to myself while maintaining my professionalism. I continue to seek conversations with my colleagues of all genders, both in hearing about and giving voice to the continued issues women of color face in student affairs and higher education profession. Too often people assume our identities define how experienced we are as professionals. I believe being of color, being young, and being a woman do not equate to being inexperienced.

REFERENCES

Blackhurst, A. E. (2000). Career satisfaction and perceptions of sex discrimination among women student affairs professionals. *NASPA Journal, 37*(2), 399–413. https://doi.org/10.2202/1949-6605.1104

Covarrubias, R., Romero, A., & Trivelli, M. (2015). Family achievement guilt and mental well-being of college students. *Journal of Child and Family Studies, 24*(7), 2031–2037. https://doi.org/10.1007/s10826-014-0003-8

Dunbar, D. P., & Kinnersley, R. T. (2011). Mentoring female administrators toward leadership success. *Delta Kappa Gamma Bulletin, 77*(3), 17–24.

Gorena, M. (1996, April). *Hispanic women in higher education administration: factors that positively influence or hinder advancement to leadership positions.* Paper presented at the meeting of the American Educational Research Association, New York, NY.

Harris Canul, K. (2003). Latina/o cultural values and the academy—Latinas navigating through the administrative role. In J. Castellanos & L. Jones (Eds.), *The majority in the minority—expanding the representation of Latina/o faculty, administrators and students in higher education* (pp. 167–175). Sterling, VA: Stylus.

Howard-Hamilton, M. F., & Williams, V. A. (1996). *Assessing the environment for women of color in student affairs* (Report No. 43). Office of Affirmative Action at Florida University. (ED398516)

Moraga, C. (2015). La güera. In C. Moraga & G. Anzaldúa (Eds.), *This bridge called my back, writings by radical women of color* (pp. 22–29). Albany: State University of New York Press.

Moraga, C., & Anzaldúa, G. (Eds.). (2015). *This bridge called my back, writings by radical women of color.* Albany: State University of New York Press.

Rodham Clinton, H. (2017). *What happened.* New York, NY: Simon & Schuster.

Sotello Viernes Turner, C. (2002). Women of color in academe: Living with multiple marginality. *The Journal of Higher Education, 73*(1), 74–93.

Sümer, H. C. (2006). Women in management: Still waiting to be full members of the club. *Sex Roles, 55*(1–2), 63–72. https://doi.org/10.1007/s11199-006-9059-2

Yakaboski, T., & Donahoo, S. (2011). In re(search) of women in student affairs administration. In P. A. Pasque & S. Errington Nicholson (Eds), *Empowering women in higher education and student affairs* (pp. 270–286). Sterling, VA: Stylus.

Yamada, M. (2015). Asian pacific American women and feminism. In C. Moraga & G. Anzaldúa (Eds.), *This bridge called my back, writings by radical women of color* (pp. 68–72). Albany: State University of New York Press.

CHAPTER 5

DEVELOPING BEST PRACTICES TO MENTOR AND EMPOWER AFRICAN AMERICAN MALE ADMINISTRATORS IN HIGHER EDUCATION

Justin Grimes
Virginia Polytechnic Institute and State University

Dallawrence Dean
University of California San Diego

Dantrayl Smith
Tarrant County College

No Ways Tired, pages 43–53
Copyright © 2019 by Information Age Publishing
All rights of reproduction in any form reserved.

Although recruiting efforts for African American males to work in higher education, particularly non-faculty, has increased over the last decade, there are challenges for African American males enduring as student affairs professionals. Thus, studies that examine methods to recruit and retain African American males are needed for the realm of higher education to continue toward having a diverse workplace. Given this premise, the purpose of this chapter is to discuss stories from African American male administrators' process of defining, identifying, and maintaining mentor relationships throughout their professional journey. The chapter will also provide some mentoring narratives and strategies for success.

Higher education has become the cornerstone for job advancement in the United States. Consequently, diverse students flood the doors of higher education looking to gain knowledge through various fields of study. As institutions of higher education seek to diversify and support their student populations, it is essential they continue to also diversify their staff in order to aid in the retention and success of their students of color. Specifically, research has shown that African American males who work in higher education aid in the success and retention of current African American male students (Harper, 2009; Harper & Davis, 2012). Although institutions have the espoused goal to have a diverse student body, many institutions fail to address their commitment to recruit and retain African American male administrators who often live and represent the diversity on campuses, outside of students (Jackson, 2002).

Mentoring has been identified as one strategy to help with recruitment and retention of students, faculty, and staff (Roberts, 2007). For the authors, there seems to be a disconnect where mentoring takes place for undergraduate African American males but stops when African American males are employees at various institutions. Given this premise, the purpose of this chapter is to provide narratives that discuss challenges, successes, definitions, and strategies African American male administrators have found to be helpful throughout their mentorship experiences as administrators.

AFRICAN AMERICAN MALES AND MENTORING

When having conversations about retention of African American males, especially on college campuses, mentoring has been identified as a successful strategy that can assist professionals of color with learning how to navigate politics, work within the institutional culture, and exceed unspoken expectations. Mentoring has also aided in increasing both the number of African American males serving as administrators as well as mentors for new professionals of color in higher education. As African American student affairs professionals, we find ourselves providing mentorship organically and through programs for students at institutions that have no formal mentorship programs in place to assist our own professional development. In a study on mentoring, Jackson (2002) revealed that establishing mentoring programs that focus on career and academic development can assist in the professional development of African American males and "sincere and seasoned mentors can challenge and support the administrator as he or she seeks to advance in their careers" (p. 13). Therefore, if mentorship has been identified as impactful for professional growth and career advancement, then we contend that it is important for African American male administrators to identify and maintain mentorship relationships.

There have been numerous studies and articles highlighting the importance of mentoring and the development of support networks in the profession of student affairs beyond entry into the profession (Batchelor, 1993; Dalton, 2003; Kelly, 1984; McDade, 1987; Roberts, 2007; Schmidt & Wolfe, 2009). For new professionals in student affairs, research has suggested that having a strong support network in place helps increase satisfaction, productivity, and active involvement in the field (Kelly, 1984; Roberts, 2007; Winston & Creamer, 1997). Building a supportive network is a significant factor we consider in mentorship.

Mentoring serves two very broad functions as professionals: career functions (i.e., coaching, providing visibility, protection, and challenging work assignments) and psychosocial functions (i.e., modeling, support, and guidance; Kram, 1985). Each of us in our professional careers pursued mentors with various social identities and professional roles different from us for advice about career options and how to navigate difficult moments. The probability of finding someone who can serve within these two functions (career and psychological) and speak to the intersection of race and gender becomes quite complicated for us as African American males. Foregoing the reality that some of our mentors, especially our African American mentors, have navigated a lot of toxicity in the field and troubling experiences navigating their careers, we hope they will have enough energy to shed some wisdom and advice to help us. In the event they are not able to, we at least learn from their experiences and see their positions as evidence that a person of color can reach their position.

The psychosocial functions of mentoring have assisted us as entry-level professionals to develop an understanding of our roles as men in non-majority male spaces. Even more, as African American males, we recognize the importance mentorship has in providing new professionals with support, guidance, and connectivity to opportunities within the field. For us, we believe that because of the scarcity of African American male professionals within our divisions, institutions, states, and regions, we are left to disaggregate our mentor functions amongst a few mentors who are more than likely not African American males. What Schmidt and Wolfe (2009) warned seems factual—there is "lack of suitable mentors for up-and-coming young professionals... can be seen as a dangerously limiting condition for the profession as well as individuals" (p. 380). In essence, we understand that there was a need for us to be clear about what type of relationship we hoped to have with a mentor considering their social identities, roles on campus, and the benefits received from their mentorship.

The benefits of mentoring are commonly facilitated by two types of mentoring—formal and informal (Kram, 1983, 1985; Packard, Walsh, & Seidenberg, 2004; Ragins & Cotton, 1999). Formal mentoring refers to organizational initiated efforts to match mentors and protégés (Eby & Lockwood, 2005). In contrast, informal mentoring occurs in a spontaneous manner where the mentor and protégé take interest in each other and a relationship subsequently develops (Chao, Walz, & Garner, 1992). When looking at these two types of mentoring through our professional experiences, we received more formal mentorship from supervisors and peers who often did not look like us, primarily because the divisions in which we worked were not very racially diverse. As a result, we chose to form informal mentorship relationships with professionals outside of our institutions, because they shared similar backgrounds and identities to us and could directly speak to the challenges of being an African American male administrator.

Despite growing mentoring literature linking mentoring experiences to essential organizational outcomes (e.g., turnover, organizational commitment), there is limited mentoring research designed to concentrate specifically on mentoring experiences among ethnic minority groups (Wood & El Mansour, 2010). The lack of ethnic minority research related to mentoring reflects a general situation in the social and behavioral sciences where ethnic minority research is uneven and undeniably inadequate (Sue, 1999). For example, there are several studies on the effects of mentoring on administrators working in higher education and strategies to retain African Americans in higher education (Calhoun & Taub, 2014), but few that focus on how mentoring relationships are developed between entry- and senior-level African Americans. Therefore, we feel research and conversation should address how African American male administrators in higher education define mentoring and the expectations of a mentoring relationship. We are choosing to share inserts from the narratives of 16 African American male's administrators working in higher education and what their experiences imply about mentoring.

Our research revealed that many of the African American male senior-level administrators mentor many entry- and mid-level administrators in higher education. However, the entry-level and mid-level professionals report they struggled to find mentors who were upper-level administrators. Since mentoring has an impact on job satisfaction and organizational commitment and institutions are looking to increase the number of African American male administrators on campus, we hope our discussion about the disconnect in mentoring relationships for this population of administrators will result in changes.

In addition, the scarcity of African American males who can or will serve as mentors presents a challenge for professionals such as us to identify and serve as mentors. The scarcity issues sometimes result in African American males competing with other African American males for same race/gender mentorship. African American male administrators seeking mentorship must first be clear about their definition of a mentor and mentor relationship before seeking out a mentor.

THE DEFINITION OF A MENTOR

We find that African American male administrators are not accustomed to expressing their thoughts, beliefs, or ideas about their experiences in student affairs because too often they have been ignored and silenced. From our research and experience, we conclude a workable definition of mentoring is a challenging/supportive learning relationship between a devoted individual who shares knowledge, experience, and wisdom with another individual who is ready and willing to benefit from this exchange, to enrich and provide direction for one's life journey.

At the core of the mentor relationship are relatability, trust, and the importance of defining what the relationship entails. It is important to remember that mentorship is not an obligation, but a relationship with either specific or fluid expectations or outcomes. According to the National Mentoring Resource Center (n.d.), mentoring relationships that are built on fundamental values of honesty and truth not only enhance the outcomes of the relationship but give the relationship strong roots to develop a lifelong mature relationship (2018). Furthermore, creating expectations and outcomes for the relationship are key to the success of a good mentorship. Not all African American males are expecting the same thing, but generally, the males who shared their viewpoints are looking for someone who is passionate about their work, dedicated to the cause, genuine, a role model, and willing to allow others to learn from their life experiences. Based on the narratives and reflections, in the next section we discuss three sub-components defined as the mentoring gap, preventing African American males from establishing strong relationships.

The Mentoring Gap

Through reflecting on our experiences and the narratives of others, we noticed how African American males go through a process of asking a set of questions about what is expected from a potential mentor, such as "Can they be helpful?" "Is this person worthy of learning from?" "Will they support me?" We also observed how we were seeking individuals with specific qualities such as observant, not exhausted or overextended, can be trusted, and is personable, honest, communicative, and transparent. These realizations led us to what we coined as the mentoring gap. The mentoring gap is made up of three major elements that have prevented us and others from identifying and establishing strong relationships. The elements are visibility, communication, and fear.

Visibility

When we entered higher education, we were seeking to establish relationships with professionals who understood what it was like to be African American, male, and a professional at our institutions of employment. One African American male talked about the unpaid labor of being both a mentor while expecting to complete one's job responsibilities and other duties as assigned. Another African American male spoke about needing somebody who can understand what he was going through with racial battle fatigue. For context, racial battle fatigue can be defined as both verbal and nonverbal microaggressions that African Americans encounter at predominantly White institutions, often leading to mental, emotional, and physical strain (Smith, Yosso, & Solórzano, 2011).

Too often, African Americans serve as the racial representatives in their office, which makes identifying mentors who have shared experiences difficult, yet essential to their success as professionals. When African American males are unable to identify a mentor at their institution, they utilize national organizations and conferences as these are systems in place to aid African American males in meeting and establishing mentoring relationships in spaces that feel more intentional.

Although these spaces provide an opportunity to connect, connections were not always made and thus, leaves African American males to identify non-African American male mentors who may only relate to them professionally and personally, but not racially or ethnically. This circumstance is important because there have been times when we observed how non-African Americans sometimes felt threatened by our presence due to society's tendency to label or view African American males as threatening, confrontational, and, in some cases, incompetent. Furthermore, the hope is for African American males to make connections at conferences, but the relationship is not always guaranteed since communication sometimes fades, leaving African American males to seek out mentorship at other places.

Time Commitment

Although the numbers of African American males entering the field of student affairs has increased and mentorship between senior level and entry/mid-level administrators is occurring, senior-level administrators often lack the necessary time to sustain their mentee-mentor relationships. We observed and experienced how personal matters, career goals, and familial responsibilities hindered a potential mentor's ability to maintain a mentee–mentor relationship. Often leaving potential mentees to feel like Peter Sullivan, who shared the status of a previous mentor:

> I have not talked to my mentor David in years. I have no idea where he is or what he's doing because it's almost to the point where David helped me and then some things happened with David and unfortunately, I wasn't able to, at the time, help David in the way that he helped me. That's sad to think about it in hindsight. (P. Sullivan, personal communication, August 11, 2014)

Peter's reflection illustrates his remorse and the value we as African American males place on mentorship, often because these opportunities are rare. For example, many African American males are often excited when opportunities to develop relationships present themselves, as illustrated by Lucas Carson:

> In my current position, our chief diversity officer is a Black man. I was like, this is awesome. I'd reach out to chief diversity officer to have a meeting or whatever and it took three months to get on his calendar. (L. Carson, personal communication, September 9, 2014)

Although Lucas was excited to meet with his institution's chief diversity officer, the amount of time it took to secure a meeting illustrates how career responsibilities often serve as a barrier to developing healthy mentoring relationships. African American males also mentioned authenticity, or a person's ability to be transparent and personable as a quality they desired in a mentor, as a relevant factor. However, when potential mentors were identified, many of them came across as uninterested. Louis Edwards, for example, described his first interaction with a prominent African American male on campus, "I met him at this lunch. He like literally was on his phone and iPad the whole time... In our conversation, it felt so political and not personal" (L. Edwards, personal communication, September 8, 2014). Additionally, African American males may feel as if potential mentors are out of touch and want to talk "to" incoming professionals as opposed to providing guidance.

Fear

In addition to visibility and communication, fear also provided insight into why we as African American males struggle to identify mentorship. Many African American males alluded to how the low amount of potential mentors at their institution leads to competition. More specifically, African American males discussed how they sometimes would forgo connecting with an African American mentor as they assumed several people would be seeking his attention. For example, Riley Jackson remarked, "It's always a minimum number and you always feel like you're competing. There's always one spot for this one or it's always one spot for this one . . . it's very rare that I see multiple African-American men at a directive level" (R. Jackson, personal communication, August 25, 2014). Similarly, participants also indicated that they often did not seek out mentors because there are "too far removed from what's real in the workplace." In other words, many African American males are unsure if they could benefit from a senior level administrator serving as their mentor. Addressing the issues presented require a set of strategies, some of which we provide below, for African American males to use in developing mentorship relationships.

STRATEGIES FOR MENTORING
FOR AFRICAN AMERICAN MALES

Mentoring African American male administrators require a familiarity with both the success and challenges of these group of male's experiences. Institutions and professionals would benefit by prioritizing mentorship as a valuable tool to recruitment, retention, and success of African American male administrators. When the authors think of strategies that can assist African American males in higher education, we reflect upon our own experiences, studies we have conducted, and our conversations with other African American males.

One strategy highlighted through shared narratives was for student affairs professionals to identify safe spaces on campus where African American males can congregate and have conversations to develop and strengthen their relationships. For example, look to explore opportunities to partner with the multicultural/intercultural offices on campus to establish safe spaces where these men can come together to dialogue about what areas they need mentoring.

Additionally, due to lack of mentors many of the participants and authors have had over their lifetime, they began to develop their own philosophy of mentoring. They also understood they may not be able to have someone directly work with them one-on-one or even in a group setting, so there is a need to take advantage of "mentoring moments" when African

American male new professionals can interact with upper-level administrators to receive advice in a quick exchange. This express method derives from entry-level African American utilizing the advice shared during those quick conversations as a mentoring moment for their career or personal pathway throughout life.

CONCLUSIONS

Mentorship is often an undervalued and unrecognized tool for an employee navigating institutional challenges and barriers. Regardless of the qualities, mentoring African American males requires a familiarity with both the success and challenges these group of men experiences. There is some discussion that African American males benefit the most from the same race and gender mentors. However, some African American males seek out mentors with different social identities, but they have very specific expectations on what those mentors can offer.

Administrators of color face greater trials that are centered on the independence or intersection of their race and gender. Aside from exposure to professional standards, mentorship can help African American male employees combat feelings of anxiety, discontent, and seclusion; while improving their personal communication and embracement of a more professional identity (Brown & Pastore, 2011; Taylor & Neimeyer, 2009). Therefore, we believe our experiences can help professionals of color define, identify, and maintain mentor relationships throughout their professional journey.

REFERENCES

Batchelor, S. W. (1993). Mentoring and self-directed learning. In M. J. Barr & Associates (Ed.), *The handbook of student affairs administration* (pp. 378–389). San Francisco, CA: Jossey-Bass.

Brown, L. E., & Pastore, D. L. (2011). Navigating a research mentorship: Recommendations for graduate students. *Future Focus (Ohio Association for Health, Physical Education, Recreation & Dance)*, *32*(2), 12–17.

Calhoun, D. W., & Taub, D. J. (2014). Exploring the gender identity roles of entry-level men in student affairs. *College Student Affairs Journal*, *32*(1), 35–51.

Chao, G. T., Walz, P. M., & Gardner, P. D. (1992). Formal and informal mentorships: A comparison on mentoring functions and contrast with non-mentored counterparts. *Personnel Psychology*, *45*(3), 619–636.

Dalton, J. C. (2003). Managing human resources. In S. R. Komives, D. B. Woodard, & Associates (Eds.), *Student services: A handbook for the profession* (pp. 397–419). San Francisco, CA: Jossey-Bass.

Eby, L. T., & Lockwood, A. (2005). Protégés and mentors' reactions to participating in formal mentoring programs: A qualitative investigation. *Journal of Vocational Behavior, 67(3)*, 441–58.

Harper, S. R. (2009). Niggers no more: A critical race counter-narrative on Black male student achievement at predominantly White colleges and universities. *International Journal of Qualitative Studies in Education (QSE), 22*(6), 697–712.

Harper, S. R., & Davis, C. H. F., III. (2012). They (don't) care about education: A counter-narrative on Black male students' responses to inequitable schooling. *Educational Foundations, 26*(1–2), 103–120.

Jackson, J. L. (2002). Retention of African American administrators at predominantly White institutions: Using professional growth factors to inform the discussion. *College and University, 78*(2), 11–16.

Kelly, K. (1984). Initiating a relationship with a mentor in student affairs. *NASPA Journal, 21*(1), 49–54.

Kram, K. E. (1983). Phases of the mentoring relationship. *Academy of Management Journal, 26*(4), 608–625.

Kram, K. E. (1985). *Mentoring at work: Developmental relationships in organizational life.* Glenview, IL: Scott Foresman.

McDade, S. A. (1987). Higher education leadership: Enhancing skills through professional development programs. *Association for the Study of Higher Education College Station, TX: ASHE-ERIC Higher Education Reports.* College Station, TX: The George Washington University.

National Mentoring Resource Center. (n.d.). *Mentoring relationship quality and characteristics.* Retrieved from https://nationalmentoringresourcecenter.org/index .php/toolkit/item/504-mentoring-relationship-quality-and-characteristics .html

Packard, B. W., Walsh, L., & Seidenberg, S. (2004). Will that be one mentor or two? A cross-sectional study of women's mentoring during college. *Mentoring and Tutoring: Partnership in Learning, 12*(1), 71–85.

Ragins, B. R., & Cotton, J. L. (1999). Mentor functions and outcomes: A comparison of men and women in formal and informal mentoring relationships. *Journal of Applied Psychology, 84*(4), 529–550.

Roberts, D. M. (2007). Preferred methods of professional development in student affairs. *NASPA Journal, 44*(3), 561–577.

Schmidt, J. A., & Wolfe, J. S. (2009). Mentor partnership: Discovery of professionalism. *NASPA Journal, 46*(3), 371–381.

Smith, W. A., Yosso, T. J., & Solórzano, D. G. (2011). Challenging racial battle fatigue on historically White campuses: A critical race examination of race-related stress. *Covert Racism, 32*, 211–238.

Sue, S. (1999). Science, ethnicity, and bias: Where have we gone wrong? *American Psychologist, 54*(12), 1070–1077.

Taylor, J. M., & Neimeyer, G. J. (2009). Graduate school mentoring in clinical, counselling, and experimental academic training programs: An exploratory study, *Counselling Psychology Quarterly, 22*(2), 257–266.

Winston, R. B., & Creamer, D. G. (1997). *Improving practices in student affairs.* San Francisco, CA: Jossey-Bass.

Wood, E. D., & El Mansour, B. (2010). Integrative literature review: Performance interventions that assist Chinese expatriates' adjustment and performance: Toward a conceptual approach. *Human Resource Development Review, 9*(2), 194–218.

CHAPTER 6

FIND A WAY OR MAKE ONE

Navigating an Intersectional Experience While Being Your Authentic Self as a New Professional of Color

Frederick V. Engram Jr.
American University

Kelli A. Perkins
University of Vermont

Michael R. Williams
Western Illinois University

Employing narrative writing combined with scholarly perspectives, this chapter seeks to provide insight to new professionals of color on how they can be true to themselves as they navigate a career in student affairs. Navigating an upwardly mobile career in higher education can often feel like a daunting task, especially when you feel like an only in your multitude of identities. The authors of this chapter provide strategies through their stories for how they have navigated careers in student affairs and higher education administration in spite of holding identities that might have kept them at the fringes.

No Ways Tired, pages 55–63
Copyright © 2019 by Information Age Publishing
All rights of reproduction in any form reserved.

Have you had the experience of being passed up for opportunity after opportunity, despite having all the necessary qualifications and it seemed like every person who received said opportunity was never a person of color? Maybe you've had a difficult time navigating your professional experience for lack of available mentors who understand and are empathetic to the marginalization that you often feel as a new professional of color. What about connectedness? Have you found your people in the workplace? Have you found your crew beyond your current professional setting who can at least help you not feel so alone in navigating this field? It can often feel like an insurmountable challenge to navigate this field as a new professional of color, especially when you look around and feel that nobody relates to you and your experiences in your everyday practice. But if you are intentional, you do not have to navigate this journey alone.

FIND AN OPPORTUNITY OR MAKE ONE: FRED'S STORY

I recall vividly what my early experiences in higher education were like. I served on teams where I literally had more experience and education than my manager and even after applying for several opportunities for promotion, I was constantly denied. On one particular occasion early in my career, I had a conversation with my supervisor and he shared that he was not oblivious to the fact that all of managers in our department were White women, even encouraging me to apply for a recent vacancy. Having a newfound confidence in the possibility of being promoted, I yet again polished off my materials and threw my hat in the ring for a position in management. And once again—I was denied the opportunity. As if things were not bad enough, I was a finalist for the position against a White male colleague who beat me out previously for a promotion. He had now received two promotions in 6 months. Nothing I could do was sufficient enough, despite already overworking myself and breaking my own rules on work–life balance.

Instead of immediately moving towards being upset and affirming for myself what I knew to be the truth of the matter, I asked my supervisor for feedback on the interview. Needless to say, he did the affirming. He told me that when I was asked about my leadership, I neglected to mention an activity I helped lead the team in that was fun and after hours. Because I neglected to mention this scenario, they did not perceive me as being ready to step into a leadership role. All the people I trained, all the hours I worked late, and because I was not enthralled with the "fun" of the office, I was deemed unworthy of promotion.

Find Your Worth, Make a Plan

Other than the fear of being terminated without a backup plan, the other frightening and detrimental word that Blacks in higher education are afraid of is being labeled angry (Kendall, 2006). Here I was in my worst professional nightmare—even after participating in the ways that I thought, according to feedback from my supervisor, were appropriate and looked highly upon—being perceived as an angry Black man. Oftentimes as people of color in higher education, we play nice in ways that hurt all of us because we make concessions so that we are not "that person." We all know that person—the one who shows up in the fullness of themselves and embraces being a "ratchademic" regardless of the space they are in. That person who will promote and support all things that expand inclusion and hold others accountable for doing the same. The person who seems angry. According to Gardner, Barrett, and Pearson (2014), African American administrators in higher education are likely to experience adjustment issues as well as difficulty navigating institutional culture and the daily dynamics of serving in academic communities that are pervasively White largely because of the harmful stereotypes that dominate the narratives around Black people in this country. Wolfe and Dilworth (2015) posited that the disparity in how African American staff are perceived in the higher education workplace has not changed much over the last 40 years.

The pervasiveness of stereotypes about people of color can negatively impact the way we feel about ourselves and our abilities. When I was noti-fied for what seemed like the hundredth time that I was passed up for a promotion, it should come as no surprise that I was experiencing imposter syndrome (Clance & Imes, 1978). People who self-declare themselves im-posters always feel at some point that someone who is high in importance or significance will find them out (Clance & Imes, 1978). I certainly was feeling that way about my situation. Maybe my supervisor was right. Maybe I was not as ready for leadership and maybe the way my supervisor viewed my work and worth was indeed correct. Feeding into White privilege and viewing the world from that paradigm can lead you to feeling brainwashed about your own self-concept (Mather, 2008).

Being a person of color is the epitome of being a survivor as your ances-tors were strong and brave. Although you cannot physically see your ances-tors or hear their voices, you must know that you are their wildest dream. You are in fact the dream and hope of the slave. Knowing this, how could you ever feel afraid to walk in your blackness? Therefore, you should dig deep within your soul as you walk into your office regardless of whatever your title is and be not ashamed of your dopeness.

And while you are being dope, make a plan. Ask for feedback, even when it stings or when the source does not seem the most valid, like the supervisor

I mentioned. As grandma said, "Eat the meat, spit out the bones." Keep your resume polished and make a clear decision about what the next step is. Finally, know that sometimes you have to just make an exit. It is okay to want to be in a professional home where you will be celebrated and valued. You are never under any obligation to stay where you do not feel wanted or where you are not growing, but make sure along the way, you are holding on to the connections that matter.

FIND A MENTOR AND BE ONE: KELLI'S STORY

According to Mosley (1980), Black women have a long history of being the only when it comes to their experiences in higher education. The physical isolation has meant that African American women often lack sufficient professional support systems and role models in the academy and are simultaneously excluded from necessary networking opportunities as well as the ability to make connections that would assist them in climbing the institutional ladder (Gregory, 1995). This recognition is not to say that men of color do not experience difficulty finding mentors, but we know that intersectionality can make this a more daunting task for women of color in the academy. White women mentors will lack the lived understanding of how race shapes Black women's experiences and Black men will lack the lived experiences with gender. To this point, it becomes difficult to develop a mentorship relationship, if at all, with a White male supervisor (Crawford & Smith, 2005).

I feel lucky that my first supervisory experience as a student affairs professional was under the tutelage of another African American woman. My experience did not necessarily begin that way, however. Initially, we clashed—a lot. I felt she was pushing me much harder than other professionals in the office, even when it was clear to everybody that I was the staff member who consistently went above and beyond. One day, I found some nerve to sit down with her and ask how I could improve. Ten years and several positions later, she is still the first person I consult when I am dealing with a professional conundrum, looking for resources, or contemplating a professional move. In her own way, she was building me up to advocate for myself in subsequent positions, which has been immensely important to my career because she was my first and last African American woman supervisor.

How do you not count mentorship out altogether if you are in a position where you might be an only or one of few people of color in your division of student affairs? Your direct supervisor is a good start. While a supervisor and a mentor are different, there are several points at which these roles can and do intersect, specifically in terms of providing feedback and perhaps connecting you to other professionals with whom you might have more shared experiences. I go into my supervisory relationships with a plan of what I am looking to get out of the experience. I ask for clear expectations of me from my supervisor. Being transparent and intentional have meant that all of my references are former supervisors who have moved up in the field (as have I) and are anywhere from assistant deans to vice presidents of student affairs. While they all have been capable of understanding the totality of my experience, because I have acquired a range of mentors, there is always someone at my disposal who will willingly assist where they can or connect me within their network.

FIND A SPONSOR OR CREATE ONE

Solidifying professional mentorship can ultimately lead to sponsorship. Hewlett (2013) described sponsorship as someone in a higher professional position within an organization who is well connected and influential, thus able to propel their protégé(s) forward professionally via their network. Oftentimes, these connections are not accessible to the protégé(s). Creating and nourishing pathways for people of color to ascend to executive levels of higher education administration will allow us to create the pathways for mentorship and eventually sponsorship for ourselves. However, we still need to remain open to receiving mentorship and sponsorship from traditionally unexpected sources, such as White men, to truly break down barriers.

January brings with it the beginning of the recruiting season for student affairs. I once had a conversation with a new professional who was in search of her second position in the field and a finalist for a position at an institution where she had connections with other people of color who were not only serving on the committee, but also held mid- and senior-level positions. She called me because she had been waiting a couple of weeks for a response and was looking for advice on how to ask where the department was in closing the search. Upon asking her if she had reached out to the professional of color she knew on the search committee, somebody she considers a friend, she responded that her friend told her that she is silent when her name comes up in conversation about the search and does not offer an opinion because she does not consider that professional. How are we supposed to get ahead if we are not helping to create pathways for each other to excel in this field and beyond (Bryant, Hilton, & Green, 2016; Gardner et al., 2014; Jean-Marie & Normore, 2010)?

Not helping each other when we are in positions to do so and holding each other to outrageous standards of how we need to show up in higher education spaces is how we directly contribute to operationalizing the notion of people of color having to be twice as good. In order to overcome some of the barriers we experience as people of color in the academy, it is important that first, we are reaching back and providing mentorship and sponsorship for other professionals of color as we climb the ranks so that secondly, we are breaking the cycle of having to be twice as a good by living in our authentic truth and normalizing our presence in higher education administration. Currently in an associate director role, I practice what I preach by making sure that when opportunities arise under my purview, I am casting the net far and wide for qualified people of color via every medium to which I have access.

FIND A COMMUNITY OR MAKE ONE: MIKE'S STORY

I often find myself spending hours in digital spaces. It could be for policy updates, educational threads, or just *tea* from my favorite Black Twitter followers. I will admit that I spend more time than necessary online, but it has allowed me to craft a digital identity and ultimately, a community that has transcended physical boundaries. Early in my social media ventures, I was using it as an escape from the realities of the world and to build an alter ego. As I continued to use social networking sites (i.e., Twitter, Instagram, and Facebook) and engage in critical racial dialogue with other professionals of color who sought out digital spaces for the same reasons as I did (mixed with an occasional shade throwing contest), I immediately noticed a shift in my process of affirming myself.

The nature of communication has changed significantly over the last few decades with the advent of the internet and mobile communication devices (Sinclair & Grieve, 2017). The prevalence of social media in higher education has led to a growing number of institutions incorporating social media in classroom pedagogy, campus programming, and student services (Chan, 2017). Social networking sites allow users to build relationships far quicker than face-to-face interactions, sometimes without the hindrance of time zones and language barriers. Online communities serve a range of purposes, from fostering a safe space to express and explore racial identity to facilitating discussions and advocacy on racial issues (Chan, 2017). In student affairs, professionals of color can often feel disconnected, especially at predominately White institutions where they could likely be an only or one of a few professionals with minoritized identities on campus. In these environments, digital communities have assisted me in fostering a sense of community when my physical location might prevented it.

When I began my doctoral journey, I was in a professional position where I was not connected to many others who had a doctoral degree or who were in a doctoral program. I announced on one of my many social media platforms that I had gotten into a Doctor of Education program and I was immediately added to a GroupMe—BLK Doctoral Students. I followed the standard protocol of introducing myself, where I would be going to school, and what I would be studying. Less than five minutes later, someone announced that they knew one person who was in my program and they added Kelli to the group. We were fast friends; not only because of our shared educational experience, but also upon discovering we were both student affairs professionals. She gave me some tips, we exchanged numbers, and I felt a new sense of confidence going into my program. Fast-forward a week—I am browsing a Facebook group for our program and notice a post of lighthearted panic about our first assignment from a brother who began the same term as me. I proceeded to tag Kelli in the post, realized she was not in that space and added her. Fred and Kelli exchanged emails and numbers and she was able to provide him with some insight for approaching the assignment that made it more manageable. Over a year later, we are still providing support for each other academically and professionally.

FIND YOUR TRIBE AND LOVE THEM HARD

As mentioned earlier, mentoring provides dual aspects of professional and psychosocial development (Kumar & Johnson, 2017). For communities of color in higher education, healing is a third aspect. The healing comes as a sense of belonging, where affirmation, value, and the ability to cope are more frequently present in the midst of what can be a higher education culture that often perpetuates oppression. Mentoring's purpose is to establish a network of support by selecting a mentor who currently exhibits habits that a protégé finds appealing for them to progress personally, educationally, or professionally. Though mentoring is an important aspect of professional life, we have to remember that we also need to spend as much time finding and nurturing healthy friendships.

While our relationship began in the mentoring realm, Fred, Kelli, and I have very much become a critical friend group. The function of a critical friend group is to develop an intimate working group where all parties share an openness to improvement, trust, respect, and a foundation in knowledge and skills in our respective profession (Curlette & Granville, 2014). We are contributing to this book because of Fred's commitment to sharing opportunities when they arise. We often tag team in our digital spaces to "school" people who need some guidance to ensure we are reaching back. We have difficult conversations about intersectionality and how we may be showing up in harmful ways in our interactions, especially because Kelli is committed to challenging us to consider our privilege every day. Most crucial to our success is each of us committing to bringing our authentic selves to these interactions, which can be difficult in a world and a profession where it oftentimes feels like we need to perform in order to be accepted. By being intentional in developing our circle, we have the ability to present our authentic selves to each other. This intentionality has made it more comfortable for us to be our authentic selves in our respective workspaces because we have crafted spaces for affirmation.

FIND LIBERATION OR BLAZE A PATH TOWARDS IT

As people of color working in student affairs, we are often reminded that our pursuits of knowledge and a more nuanced understanding of how to transform the world via education is not just for us individually, but all the people who we will touch directly and indirectly. In our professional roles, we speak not only for ourselves but aim to center the voices of others who have been historically and institutionally marginalized, disenfranchised, and disempowered. According to Bailey and Grautam (2015), an educational leader has a primary responsibility to act and be aware that a lack of action will have real costs for real people.

The process of liberation from oppressive systems is a shared one. It does not belong solely to the one needing freedom or the one providing the means to freedom; but it is a process in which we have a collective responsibility so that freedom may be fully actualized. Many people of color enter the field of student affairs because of the belief that education is a means to freedom and acknowledge this is "a field in which we all labor" (hooks, 1994, p. 14). According to Flinders and Thornton (2013), full liberation is found in the collective and it is the responsibility of us in the academy to call the totality of humanity to the table and facilitate the dialogues and interactions that will ultimately lead to freedom.

But before you are able to fully engage in honoring the collective, you must engage in the process of honoring and liberating yourself. hooks (1994) informed us that an engaged pedagogy reinforces well-being and the wholeness of the educator—mind, body, and soul. A student affairs professional living in their truth is one who undertakes "practice through contemplation" and seeks to be whole in order to help others find the agency to engage in their own process of becoming whole and ultimately free (p. 15). It is this process of self-actualization that keeps us and the field of student affairs humble, which is a necessity for dialogue towards liberation to exist (Flinders & Thornton, 2013). In other words—show up, show out, and be your full self whether you are a "ratchademic," can go from the block to the boardroom, or are the awkward Black girl. Take care of each other. Reach back as you climb. Find community by any means necessary—your digital spaces do not just need to be places you go to escape everyday reality. The advancement of people of color in this field, and ultimately future generations of students of color, depends on you.

REFERENCES

Bailey, S., & Gautam, C. (2015). A philosophical twist to the scholar-practitioner tradition. *Education Research and Perspectives: An International Journal, 42*, 556–581.

Bryant, C. J., Hilton, A. A., & Green-Powell, P. A. (2015). African American doctoral scholars' and fellows' professional development mentoring experiences toward higher education professorship. *Journal of Research Initiatives, 1*(3), 1–10.

Clance, P. R., & Imes, S. (1978). The imposter phenomenon in high achieving women: Dynamics and therapeutic intervention. *Psychotherapy Theory, Research and Practice Volume, 15*(3), 1–8.

Crawford, K., & Smith, D. (2005). The we and the us: Mentoring African American women. *Journal of Black Studies, 36*(1), 52–67.

Curlette, W. L., & Granville, H. G. (2014). The four crucial Cs in critical friends groups. *Journal of Individual Psychology, 70*(1), 21–30.

Flinders, D. J., & Thornton, S. J. (Eds.) (2013). *The curriculum studies reader.* New York, NY: Routledge.

Gardner, Jr., L., Barrett, T. G., & Pearson, L. C. (2014). African American administrators at PWIs: Enablers of and barriers to career success. *Journal of Diversity in Higher Education, 7*(4), 235–251.

Gregory, S. T. (1995). *Black women in the academy: The secrets to success and achievement.* New York, NY: University Press of America.

Hewlett, S. (2013). *Forget a mentor: Find a sponsor.* Boston, MA: Harvard Business Review Press.

hooks, b. (1994). *Teaching to transgress: Education as the practice of freedom.* New York, NY: Routledge.

Jean-Marie, G., & Normore, A. (2010). The impact of relational leadership, social justice and spirituality among female secondary school leaders. *International Journal of Urban Educational Leadership, 4*, 22–43.

Kendall, F. E. (2006). *Understanding white privilege: Creating pathways to authentic relationships across race.* New York, NY: Routledge.

Kumar, S., & Johnson, M. (2017). Mentoring doctoral students online: Mentor strategies and challenges. *Mentoring & Tutoring: Partnership in Learning, 25*(2), 202–222.

Mather, S. (2008). Social experiment wolves in social justice sheepskins: Defanging inquisitional variants of whiteness theory via critical realism. *Philosophy of Education,* 81–90. Retrieved from https://pdfs.semanticscholar.org/cb25/eca07daa7f6d066b6b8dbc6436ce4f35119e.pdf?_ga%3D2.137846192.1610693456.1560958164-613638772.1560958164&sa=D&source=hangouts&ust=1561046187407000&usg=AFQjCNFwbsoREi2zlAXVT6YPTesfIKg_lQ

Mosley, M. H. (1980). Black women administrators in higher education: An endangered species. *Journal of Black Studies, 10*(3), 295–310.

Sinclair, T. J., & Grieve, R. (2017). Facebook as a source of social connectedness in older adults. *Computers in Human Behavior, 66*, 363–369.

Wolfe, B. L., & Dilworth, P. P. (2015). Transitioning normalcy: Organizational culture, African American administrators, and diversity leadership in higher education. *Review of Educational Research, 85*(4), 667–697.

CHAPTER 7

DOING THE WORK

A College Administrator's Journey of Self-Discovery

Karen F. Jackson
Georgia Gwinnett College

Student affairs professionals play a vital role in student success as their work supports students' mental, emotional, physical, spiritual, and intellectual development. Because their identity, values, and beliefs affect how they view others and the decisions they make in their professional lives, student affairs staff must continually examine their belief systems to ensure they are effectively supporting their students. This essay discusses one administrator's journey of self-discovery that helped her become more effective in her job and a better advocate for her students.

As colleges and universities are more diverse and work to become more student centered, student affairs professionals are playing a significant role in the transformation of higher education. Student affairs professionals' work enhances the student experience and supports the overall mission of these institutions. Vincent Tinto's (1975) seminal work, *Dropout from Higher Education: A Theoretical Synthesis of Recent Research*, indicated that

No Ways Tired, pages 65–73
Copyright © 2019 by Information Age Publishing
All rights of reproduction in any form reserved.

social integration plays a critical role in the retention, progression, and graduation of college students. This impact is particularly notable for underrepresented and underserved students (Webber & Ehrenberg, 2010). Tinto further notes that information/advice, support, involvement, and learning are four significant institutional conditions that affect retention (Tinto, 1999). Student affairs professionals make substantial contributions in all these areas.

Our expanding roles provide us with greater opportunities to directly impact students through daily interactions and mentoring (formal and informal) and by developing campus policies and programs that promote institutional change. The decisions we make about such policies and programs, and even how we interact with students and campus partners, are guided by our own identities, values, and beliefs. These factors influence the assumptions we have about our students, our work environment, and most importantly, ourselves. They also affect our thoughts about what we can accomplish in our professional roles. Therefore, it is paramount that we engage in continual reflection to assess our values and belief systems. Additionally, we must be conscious of the environments in which we work and understand how our identity guides us as we navigate these settings. This chapter will chronicle my journey of coming to terms with my own identity and how doing so helped me to better serve my students.

BEHIND THE MASK

Black women's lives are a series of negotiations that aim to reconcile the contradictions separating our own internally defined images of self as African-American women with our objectification as the Other.

—Collins, 2000, p. 99

Like many new student affairs professionals, I was ready to change the world when I started my first job in higher education. I read books on student development theory, completed internships, and attended several professional conferences. I had many ideas about programs for students and planned my professional trajectory. However, although I spent a lot of time developing my professional skills, I did not put much effort into cultivating a strong belief system and positive self-image. Nor did I understand how my beliefs and values were connected to how I walked through the professional world. As the quote above implies, how we, African American women, view ourselves often conflicts with the images society displays to us. These marginalized reflections are usually based on a Eurocentric worldview and attempt to relegate the African American's role in society. Consequently, identity development for African Americans can be a challenging process. Cross

(1971) identifies five stages of African American identity development in which individuals progress from accepting Eurocentric-based values and beliefs to becoming secure with their own racial identity and being committed to addressing the issues of their own race. It became clear that by the time I started my career, I had not progressed past the first phase of Cross' model and accepted society's reflection of "the other" as my identity.

My decision to pursue a career in higher education was partially the result of a positive college experience and my desire to remain in what I perceived as a safe and comfortable environment. I was also influenced by the student affairs professionals who supported me while I was in college. I benefited immensely from the dedicated support of the African American student affairs staff who acted as mentors to not only me, but all the African American students on campus. They displayed a genuine interest in our well-being and provided programs and other resources they believed would help us thrive. Equally important was that they appeared to enjoy what they were doing, which was a key factor in my career exploration. I enjoyed my college years and seeing my mentors demonstrate that same joy and enthusiasm in their professional roles solidified my career choice.

When I started my first job in higher education, I expected to have the same euphoric feelings I experienced as an undergraduate. Even though I was the only African American in my office, I did not think my race or gender would be a factor in my career progression. Instead, I believed excellent work ethic and integrity would propel my career. Thank you notes from my supervisor made me feel appreciated for the work I was doing and I was frequently invited to socialize with my colleagues outside of work, which provided an erroneous sense of acceptance. I was even more convinced that although racism did exist, society had gotten better and people of color were judged on their merit and rewarded accordingly.

Initially, I was satisfied with the way my career was progressing, but it did not take long for me to have experiences that demonstrated my race and gender might preclude me from the same benefits and respect my White male peers received. I began to notice my colleagues' verbal microaggressions like, "They are so articulate" and "I don't see color" when talking about African American students. I heard them reference groups of black and brown female students as "sistahs." Although I knew this was wrong, I still found it hard to acknowledge that some of my colleagues might be racist. Even when I found out a less experienced White male colleague who I trained was making more money than me, I could not fathom that I was being discriminated against. I had been doing the job of two people since my first day, exceeded my performance goals, and had been, what I thought, the model employee. Surely, my supervisor did not accept the sexist view that a man's work was more valuable than a woman's work or that my skin color made me less deserving. I convinced myself that my colleague was a better negotiator. Then I remembered that I had not been given the opportunity to negotiate. Even worse, I did not think I had the right to negotiate and had to be given permission to do so.

There were other incidents involving a White male supervisor who would say things to me like "I like your hair better this way. It's more controlled," referring to the braided hairstyle I was wearing versus the short afro I had previously worn. On one occasion he asked, "How is it that you are even here? I mean, you're a Black woman from a low-income family and neither of your parents went to college." I wanted to say,

> I'm smart and I work hard. My working-class parents valued education just as much as your White college educated parents. And even though they were born into a society where it was legal to discriminate against African Americans, my parents had the work ethic, fortitude, and value system to get me here.

But I did not. I found it easier to focus my weak retort on my parents' value of education and then make excuses for his behavior. I rationalized his actions by telling myself, "He doesn't know any better." Additionally, I foolishly attributed his comments to his social awkwardness and believed it was my job to educate him because he had never really been around Black people before. In the end, I did not make any earnest effort to change his perspective. Instead, I began to plan my exit.

These occurrences demonstrate how I minimized incidents of racism that I personally experienced and continued to blindly subscribe to the ideals of meritocracy (Bonilla-Silva, 2006). It was particularly problematic in my chosen profession because if I allowed myself to be disrespected by my colleagues, how could I stand up for my students? When student affairs professionals of color internalize the impact of colorblind racism, they limit not only their professional growth but also the impact they can have on the lives of students they serve. I now realize that during this time in my career, my own identity and belief system directed my focus to helping students navigate the landscape of higher education when I should have focused on changing the landscape to better serve the students.

DOING THE WORK

While these examples do not define my entire career, they were pivotal points along my professional journey that evoked cognitive dissonance that forced me to begin the process of reconciling my personal values and what I needed to do in my career. I knew what I was observing and experiencing was demeaning and racist, but until then, I had not been compelled to do anything about it. My reaction to these incidents was inaction and a willingness to "stay in my place" and accept the inferior value that had been ascribed to me. Eventually, I realized that I could not have this mindset and be effective in my chosen career. It was not possible for me to help students reach their potential and strive for excellence if I had a limiting view of myself. I had to reclaim my agency and define my own identity and self-worth if I was going to live a meaningful life and have a fulfilling and purposeful career. It was time for me to take inventory of what I believed about myself, higher education, and my role in the profession.

My first step was to reflect and gain a true understanding of what I believed about myself and how I developed those beliefs. This phase prompted me to consider the things I heard and witnessed growing up. My parents were very encouraging and always told me I could do and be anything if I worked hard and received an education, but they did not believe this for themselves. Although there was distrust of the dominant culture, they still believed "White was right." They never said this to me directly, but the message made its way into my subconscious as I watched the way they humbled themselves around White people and overheard their conversations about race. They were not aware that their actions and conversations were indirectly communicating such a negative message to me and I am not sure if they even recognized the negativity to be a part of their own belief systems. Nonetheless, I understand this impacted how I felt about myself and race relations.

The seeds planted during my childhood became fast growing weeds when I got to college. When I took an honest look at my undergraduate college experience, I began to understand that mine was an insulated experience. Although I attended a predominantly White institution (PWI), I only socialized with other African American students and joined organizations associated with Black causes. The decision to "remain with my own" was intentional and helped me cope with the imposter syndrome (Clance & Imes, 1978). Moreover, as a first-generation African American student at a PWI, there were many things I did not know and because I had preconceived notions about what others thought about me and my lack of cultural capital (Bourdieu, 1986), I was not going to put myself in situations that might confirm that I did not belong. I was even guarded in some of my interactions with other African American students for fear of being "found out." I carried this burden into my career and it reared its head every time I wanted to voice my opinion or take advantage of an opportunity. Instead, I sat quietly and went along with the crowd or watched someone else take a chance on a new professional prospect.

Uncovering these things about myself was not easy and after doing so, I had to figure how I could use this information to reconstruct my belief system. I always encouraged my students to ask for help and I knew that I needed to do the same. During the second part of this process, I sought the assistance of those I believed were courageous and living authentically.

Some of them worked in higher education, others did not, but they all projected a positive self-image. Many of the conversations centered on how they were able to be comfortable in their own skin and their experiences navigating institutional racism and gender bias while being a catalyst for institutional change through their life's work. We talked about what it meant to live authentically and to truly embrace who you are. In addition to listening to their sage advice, when the opportunity was presented, I carefully observed them in professional settings to see how they comfortably and confidently displayed their true selves. They suggested readings about social and cultural matters including class, identity, and race theory. Much of what I was discussing, observing, and reading was information that I had encountered before, but I had just arrived at a place where I could receive it. I realized that while I thought my previous belief system made it easier for me to operate safely within the higher education system, it stifled my professional growth, limited how I served my students, and decreased opportunities to influence institutional culture in ways that would be more inclusive and supportive of students, faculty, and staff. Playing it safe and staying in my place resulted in many missed opportunities for me to openly question adverse policies and practices and to offer more inclusive solutions that would benefit my students' well-being and academic success. Moreover, this action would have made me more confident in who I was as a person and what I could accomplish professionally.

REEMERGENCE

As I began to internalize all I learned by dispelling the negative beliefs I had about myself, I noticed a shift in how I moved through the world. I interacted with others with more confidence and a greater sense of purpose. I became less hesitant to share my opinions and question policies and practices that were not inclusive or hindered student progress. My focus was no longer on just the equal treatment of students but included advocating for equity so that all students could take advantage of the opportunities offered. I also began to share my story with my colleagues to help them dispel some of the assumptions they had about our students whose background was different from theirs. Before, I would have been embarrassed to talk about the fact that neither of my parents had a high school diploma or that my socioeconomic status qualified me for free lunch in elementary school. I came to realize those things are part of my story but do not define my destiny. And if I could get my colleagues to understand that about me, perhaps they would understand that about our students and work to develop an inclusive institutional culture in which all students can thrive.

Although this process was uncomfortable, jarring, and sometimes painful, it was necessary if I was going to be comfortable with who I am and operate in my own personal and professional truths. I recognize that I now bring valuable experience, knowledge, and compassion to the table and no longer "stay in my place." I am not hesitant to question policies and programs that might hinder the progress of marginalized students because I understand the need for them. I can fully appreciate my gifts and talents and recognize how I contribute to my profession. Additionally, focusing on my purpose and radiating an authentic self-image has also helped to advance my career. I have received state and national recognition for my work and I am frequently asked to participate in projects aimed at transforming the lives of students. However, the most rewarding accolades continue to come from seeing my students succeed.

CONCLUSION

Considering the changing landscape of higher education, recurrent examinations of our belief systems within the contexts of our professional roles and responsibilities are necessary for us to be effective in our careers. Examples of questions we can use to reflect include:

- What are my values and beliefs as they relate to my identity? To my career?
- What experiences have shaped my values and beliefs?
- What is the institutional culture and is it congruent with my beliefs and values?
- What assumptions do I make about my students?
- How have my values and beliefs contributed to the decisions I've made in my position?

Taking the time to reflect also gives us the opportunity to celebrate our accomplishments, which is necessary to keep us motivated. Most of us in student affairs enter the field because we want to make a difference in the lives of young adults. We are not seeking awards and recognition. Our reward often comes in the form of seeing a student accomplish a goal like improving their GPA, joining an organization, or graduating. Sometimes just a conversation with an alumnus can remind us that we made difference and that is all the acknowledgement we need. Taking the time to recognize that you are impacting lives can give you the inspiration you need to continue the work.

In addition to continuous self-reflection, we need to identify partners who can support us in our professional journeys. Sometimes institutions will offer formal mentoring programs for new staff. In addition to providing a point of contact with whom you can discuss professional issues, these programs can be an effective way to learn more about the institutional culture, which will help you navigate the environment. Even if you are part of a formal mentoring program, you should also create your own "board of directors." This is a group of individuals with whom you can have conversations about your career, values, and beliefs. These people can be mentors, friends, or colleagues. The most important criteria are that they are honest with you and hold you accountable about your decisions, goals, and action plans. They need to be willing to challenge you to think deeply and help you understand the connections between your decisions and beliefs. They need to be unafraid to tell you when you are wrong and help you understand why. They must be people you trust enough to be open and honest with and be willing to learn from. Your board members must also have the time to commit to supporting you. You should be clear about your needs when asking them to serve. Finally, don't be afraid to "retire" your board members. Some relationships are not meant to last forever. A new position, new school, or new experience might require the expertise or wisdom not represented on the board.

How we perform our job is directly connected to our personal beliefs, values, and identity. As student affairs professionals, this connection manifests in the programs and policies we develop, implement, and enforce. As such, it is imperative for us to understand who we are and how we came to be. To not engage in this type of self-reflection would not only limit our personal and professional growth, it would limit the success of our students and would be a disservice to those who entrusted us with their development.

REFERENCES

Bonilla-Silva, E. (2006) *Racism without racists: Color-blind racism and the persistence of racial inequality in the United States* (2nd ed.). Lanham, MD: Rowman & Littlefield.

Bourdieu, P. (1986). The forms of capital. In J. G. Richardson (Ed.), *Handbook of theory and research for the sociology of education* (pp. 241–258). New York, NY: Greenwood.

Clance, P. R., & Imes, S. A. (1978). The imposter phenomenon in high achieving women: Dynamics and therapeutic intervention. *Psychotherapy: Theory, Research & Practice, 15*(3), 241–247.

Collins, P. H. (2000). *Black feminist thought: Knowledge, consciousness, and the politics of empowerment.* New York, NY: Routledge.

Cross, W. (1971). The Negro-to-Black conversion experience. *Black World, 20*(9), 3–27.

Tinto, V. (1975). Dropout from higher education: A theoretical synthesis of recent research. *Review of Educational Research, 45*(1), 89–125.

Tinto, V. (1999). Taking retention seriously: Rethinking the first year of college. *NACADA Journal, 19*(2), 5–9. Retrieved from https://doi.org/10.12930/0271 -9517-19.2.5

Webber, D., &. Ehrenberg, R. G (2010, April 15). *Do expenditures other than instructional expenditures affect graduation and persistence rates in American higher education?* Retrieved from Cornell University, School of Industrial and Labor Relations site: http://digitalcommons.ilr.cornell.edu/workingpapers/129/

CHAPTER 8

ESCAPE, ADAPT, AND THRIVE

In Search of the Promised Land

Melvin (Jai) Jackson
North Carolina State University

The journey for professionals of color in higher education is often faced with everyday struggles of working twice as hard as the majority in order to gain half as much. The everyday challenge to thrive in these institutionally xenophobic educational environments is a constant threat to the physical and psychological well-being of professionals of color. This chapter will explore the narrative of a mid-level professional who experienced the stress and used it to transition towards success and the path taken to outlasting the hate and thriving as a professional of color in an international setting abroad. From navigating the microaggressions and assaults of the American higher education system to seeking and securing employment abroad.

A fresh-faced Black professional enters the fast-paced environment of American higher education at a predominantly White institution. Without warning, I became engulfed in an all too familiar sea of White faces, donning white collars and Black hands dry and chapped from hard days of manual labor. Upon entry to this ivory tower, the smiles seemed genuine and the invitations honest and sincere. As days became weeks, I was mentored by

No Ways Tired, pages 75–84
Copyright © 2019 by Information Age Publishing
All rights of reproduction in any form reserved.

supervisors who challenged me to change the office dynamic, help to promote diversity, and serve as a mentor to the sparsely populated and, often, denigrated Black youth working these academic fields. I, too, worked those academic fields, just to glimpse the ivory tower of education only to escape into a life of professional tokenism. Reality struck when I understood I was hired not because of the content of my character but for the color of my skin. I realized that the facade of equity promoted in interviews, conversations, and commonly celebrated on webpages was nothing more than a rouse. The covert racism that existed throughout American society was alive and overtly engrained on campus. How does one escape the institutional racism that echoes through the ivory tower of higher education when it is also engrained in American society and culture? To escape a people united by hatred, I worked to escape the confines of American culture that built these racist foundations in favor of a land of familiar faces. Unfortunately, I realized that while the borders of the United States are tangible and deterred by the ocean waves, the reality is that institutional racism was a global pandemic. I understood the infectious nature of racism and though I transitioned abroad and into the faculty ranks, the viral nature of intolerance was pervasive and widespread.

The narrative above features an increasingly familiar experience of Black higher education professionals who aspire to thrive in a society that does not respect nor appreciate their Black bodies. The dialogue that exists to support this narrative discloses a culture of institutionalized racism that is profoundly fostered throughout our institutions of higher learning. For Black student affairs professionals working at predominantly White colleges and universities in the United States, an unwavering oppressive sentiment envelops the environment around many campuses (Smith, Allen, & Danley, 2007). As a Black higher education professional, I unknowingly thrust myself into the covertly racialized field only to be denigrated, paraded, and cast away. I escaped from the institutionally racist ivory towers of American higher education because the adaptation that was required for my success would have cost me my dignity and my values. I attempted to thrive by changing the environment that tried to break me, only to understand that the racist and challenging ideals perpetuated in the American system were infectious and itinerant. Those very ideals were not limited to the expanse of the United States; their covert racist misandry extended throughout the increasingly colonized world.

As a Black man coexisting in White America, my stress extended beyond environmental and became a natural aspect consequence of life. Living in a world that forces me to divide my consciousness into individual compartments has been a battle rife with pyrrhic victories and the casualties easily began to mount. The choice to pursue professional and personal opportunities abroad was fueled by the desire to circumvent both visible and invisible glass ceilings that exist in American higher education.

This chapter will explore the experiences of a Black male mid-level higher education professional working in an international setting who is striving to succeed amidst an unjust system of institutionalized racism. While international higher education may hold many benefits of wanderlust and financial security, there are challenges one will encounter and ways to overcome these challenges. The narrative will detail how I attempted to escape the tyranny of a higher education system marred in institutionalized racism, my attempts to adapt to a new environment with its own hidden issues of racial superiority and microaggressions/assaults, and steps employed in order to overcome and thrive in this environment. Additionally, I will explore practices to overcome the shock of institutionalized racism in a setting where, though individuals may have a familiar melanin tint, they have their own agendas.

INSTITUTIONALIZED RACISM OF HIGHER EDUCATION

Within the U.S. higher education system, xenophobia exists as a set of communally organized practices, attitudes, and mindsets that deny persons of color the benefits that are offered to Whites (Smith, 2010). An environment of bigotry was a regular occurrence as a higher education professional working at predominantly White institutions (PWIs). Race and the divisive constructions that compartmentalize and categorize individuals were instituted to delineate those who were perceived to be superior over another race of people (Solorzano, Ceja, & Yosso, 2000). As a Black staff member working white collar jobs at various higher education institutions, I was allowed to partake in the "water cooler" conversations of my White colleagues but never truly had a "seat at the table." The majority of Black employees I encountered served in positions that echoed times of servitude: cleaning buildings, maintaining order as campus security (overseers), or serving food to White students who thought nothing more of them than expendable labor. The institutionalized disdain for Black bodies and Black voices exists to subordinate and tyrannize these people regardless of their job classification or position power.

Institutionalized racism encapsulated many aspects of university life including hiring practices. For years, tokenism at these PWIs was represented in countless brochures handed out in droves to potential new students. Front pages, plastered with a diverse array of students representing the seemingly thriving diverse population that existed on the campus, became the cornerstone for the promotion of tokenism amongst the diverse populations. Not limited to students, Black and Brown faces are commonly represented on hiring committees as a means for enticing unsuspecting prey to these institutions to meet institutional quotas for diversity. In my career, I was not immune to serving as the token Black hire thrust in front of wealthy alumni and anxious diverse students. I was not exempt from serving as the advisor to the Black student clubs. I was nothing more than a glorified token Black higher education professional serving my purpose until I grew less jaded.

INSTITUTIONALIZED RACISM ABROAD

Microaggressions are subtle incidents or actions that are discriminatory towards marginalized groups of people (Smith, Hung, & Franklin, 2011). The microaggressions I experienced as a higher education professional extended beyond the American higher education system and infected everyday life. These instances served as continuous reminders of my plight and place in a covertly racist country.

In the Middle East, countries are rife with individuals who represent marginalized populations. When many Middle Eastern countries began building a robust tertiary education system, they modeled their institutions after the American system (Alhebsi, Pettaway, & Waller, 2015). This modeling came not only with the frameworks for liberal arts, STEM, and post-secondary education, but the foundational structures of institutionalized racism were also integrated into the policies and procedures (Bourne, 2001). The history of higher education in the United States is built on racist ideals and principles that are perpetuated in all aspects of the American higher education system (Ladson-Billings, 2013; Leonardo, 2009). As White administrators are sought to build a system of education abroad that equates or exceeds standards of the American education system, they often unintentionally bring about the perpetuation of institutionalized racism (Bonilla-Silva, 2012; Bourne, 2001).

The "White mentality" caused numerous bouts of racial battle fatigue (RBF), a psychological state in which an individual experiences increased anxiety, frustration, anger, and depression as a result of micro assaults and microaggressions (Stevenson, 2013). Upon deciding to leave the United States for a professional and personal quest for enlightenment and equity, I believed the decision to move to the Middle East would grant me solace. A sea of familiar Black and Brown faces and a perceived feeling of equality was what I believed would be waiting for me at the end of a 15-hour flight. After orienting and becoming better acclimated to the cultural and societal changes, I began my quest for understanding how the higher education environment in the Middle East would differ from that of the United States, only to realize that racism is a highly contagious and pervasive virus with roots throughout the colonized world (Smith, Yosso, & Solorzano, 2006). Questions of my heritage often served as ice breakers in many conversations—"Where are you from? Where is your family from? Where did you come from?" There was pride and arrogance associated with individuals of white skin originating in white monarchies. I understood that the melanin of my skin had greater influence than the extent of my professional and academic knowledge. Many of my White colleagues would play a one-sided racist game of questioning the academic rigor of my degrees in addition to my "Blackness." Naturally, I identify as a Black American man, but I would consistently be met with the question from staff, faculty, and students alike of, "Where are you REALLY from?" Such a question went beyond my North Carolina native accent and straight to my perceived lack of heritage and belonging in white America. The perceptions of these questions by my White and "White-aspiring" colleagues provided a sense of superiority at the expense of denigrating and belittling my worth as a Black man. In one situation, a colleague with Kurdish heritage and British citizenship scoffed at the idea that she and I had experienced equally stressful histories regarding the plight of our respective peoples. She felt her identity was singularly isolated to the origination of her passport and the supremacy of her country. This instance and a flurry of other microaggressions and micro assaults would further exacerbate my RBF.

BLACK, AGGRESSED, UNITED

Following my collapse from countless covert and overt acts of microaggressions and micro assaults within various student affairs units, I began the process of reconnecting with faculty and students of color. To reify my foundation and build a more firmly placed scaffolding for myself and other people of color experiencing similar feelings of fatigue, I offered myself as a resource. Within the higher education landscape at a PWI, I observed the creation and assembly of Black cultural groups that served as formal representation and informal support networks that were much needed (Carter, 2009; Jackson, 2017). Because these feelings of isolation and aggression were not limited to one demographic of campus stakeholder, these feelings were a natural unifier that served as the motivator for the creation of support networks for Blacks. It is absolutely necessary for Black students to be provided with supportive relationships with administrators and faculty that look like them (Harper, 2009). Black professionals at PWIs are also in need of networks that offer support and engagement to provide a safe space from the storm of microaggressions and micro assaults they often experience (Smith, Hung, & Franklin, 2012).

The institutionalized racism African Americans experience is engrained in the higher education institution and subconsciously indoctrinated into the students (Harper, 2009; Solorzano et al., 2000). In order to be accepted by the dominant White culture, African Americans must adapt to the surroundings and cultural norms instilled in the institutionally racialized culture of campus; adopt a lifestyle and understanding of their place in the hierarchy of the racial climate; and integrate via force into established norms and constructs of PWIs (Bourne, 2001; Smith, 2010) or risk continued anxiety, stress, and isolation (Thomas, 1981). Isolated racialized microaggressions may seem harmless, but the cumulative burden of a lifetime of microaggressions can theoretically contribute to diminished mortality, augmented morbidity, and flattened confidence (Smith, Allen, & Danley, 2007). As a means for preserving my sanity and mortality, I knew that I needed to look for other opportunities for personal and professional success.

PURSUING HIGHER EDUCATION EMPLOYMENT ABROAD

For those interested in pursuing employment in higher education abroad, there are several things to consider before making the decision to uproot your life as well as all that is familiar and the norm for you and your family. I contend there are several barriers to seeking international employment for professionals of color including cultural, professional, and personal. To address the cultural barrier, you should truly understand the culture(s) in which you are seeking employment. Are the values and beliefs congruent with your own system of values and cultural beliefs and norms? To enter a culture that is unfamiliar to your own can cause feelings of unacceptance and psychological stress. From a professional perspective, you must understand that the common higher education practice of continuous movement from university to university can be perceived as being non-committed by institutions abroad. Additionally, when hired by institutions abroad, professionals often commit to multi-year employment contracts that sometimes include strict penalties for breaking contracts early. Increasingly, professionals who experience wanderlust perceive that working abroad in a central locale like the Middle East will afford them the opportunity to travel to various destinations around the world as they please. However, travel can be limited due to employment policies. Personal barriers include abandoning family, friends, and familiarity. Upon making the decision to pursue employment abroad, you are met with the tough decision to leave your family and friends behind for your personal/professional gain. This circumstance is difficult because you are thousands of miles away and potentially without the close support network you have established. While communicating via technology can make this decision easier, as a professional, you must be comfortable and confident to establish new systems of support and guidance. In addition, though technology may help to ease the transition and feelings of homesickness, some VoIP (voice and video) may be illegal and a danger to use.

Regardless of the barriers, thousands of individuals vacate the relative comfort of their everyday American lives with the goal of new experiences. The unfamiliarity that comes with living in a new country can be overwhelming. A land of new faces, a new way of life, and a potential language barrier can be stressful and daunting. Such circumstances can cause professionals abroad to face the dilemma of acclimation or assimilation. Acclimating and assimilating to new cultures can be difficult for those who are accustomed to their domestic life at home. The budding professional abroad needs to decide if their goal was to acclimate by living their life alongside the existing culture and community or rather assimilate and truly immerse themselves into the culture and become a cultural member of the country. Your interest in positions abroad signifies that you (hopefully) have a respect and appreciation for cultures and people unlike yourself. Trust the process and remember to use your personal and professional network as your board of advisors.

For higher education professionals of color, employment abroad provides exciting opportunities for professional satisfaction and personal gain. Subsequently, if there is an interest in an international opportunity, one must prudently navigate the process to search and secure a professionally lucrative prospect. For those who choose to undertake the employment abroad process, the following suggestions can aid in the job search.

- Similar to a job search in the United States, utilize a variety of methods to seek open positions, including job search sites, email lists, word of mouth, direct university searches, utilizing connections, and so forth. It's not simply what you know but who you know.
- Reach out to professional and social networks to connect with those who may already be established in a university, country, or region abroad of interest. Use their experiences, opinions, and access to bolster your decision to move forward, but remember that ultimately, the experience may vary from that of your colleague(s).

THE WAITING GAME

International employment takes time. Let's suppose you have applied for a position(s) and submitted all required documentation and supporting credentials and it has been over a month since the deadline passed. It is okay to follow up with the university but realize there are several clearances and approvals that must be secured before the institution can move forward with your potential candidacy. Moreover, be productive and do your homework on the institutions in addition to the respective cultures and communities. Know what you are getting yourself into when working abroad. Exotic destinations look great on television and in magazines, but the life of a tourist is much more different than the life of a resident.

THE INTERVIEW

The first rule of international interviews is flexibility. The time difference can make for some interesting interview times. Remember, you are the candidate and you want the job; so be willing to wake up extra early for that 4:00 a.m. video interview. Accept that communication is key, and you will need to understand that those interviewing you may represent a multitude of languages and cultures. English is a great unifier of cultures and countries, but it is not the first language of all those you may encounter. During the interview, speak slowly and clearly, listen intently, sparingly using terminology that you may think is common and ask for clarification if you are having a difficult time understanding. You should also be prepared to ask questions that range from the professional culture and community to general living and life outside of work.

ACCEPTING THE OFFER

Negotiations are contingent on your position, the location of the job, and the organizational structure/makeup (i.e., governmental, nongovernmental, private). Before you sign the contract, confirm every detail and ask clarifying questions, especially since many contracts are long-term and leave no room for negotiations after all documents are signed and submitted. Recognize your contract terms explicitly and read the fine print. For example, holidays for you may not be holidays for your organization.

Moving across the globe can be confusing, exciting, and stressful. Consider the following in your decision-making process: professional development, social support, lifestyle choices, and societal/cultural norms. Things to consider after you accept an offer include living arrangements, transportation, pets, spouse/kids, personal/professional networks, entertainment, and so on.

CONCLUSION

The victory of surviving the psychological stress of being a student affairs professional of color in the United States and transitioning to a successful career abroad has been an inspirational undertaking. I was once ridiculed for the opportunities I chose to seek to aide in my success and pulled into a seemingly uphill battle and struggle; but eventually, I succeeded as a Black male higher education professional. The opportunities for growth through international experiences for people of color in higher education are plentiful and a professional of color should consider continuing their professional, personal, and educational ascension through an international experience. For many professionals who are successful in transitioning to an international environment that is rich with diversity, the experience can be eye opening, revitalizing, and life changing.

REFERENCES

Alhebsi, A., Pettaway, L., & Waller, L. (2015). A history of education in the United Arab Emirates and Trucial Shiekdoms. *The Global eLearning Journal, 4*(1), 1–6.

Bonilla-Silva, E. (2012). The invisible weight of whiteness: The racial grammar of everyday life in America. *Michigan Sociological Review*, 1–15.

Bourne, J. (2001). The life and times of institutionalized racism. *Race Class, 43*(2), 7–22.

Carter, P. L. (2009) Equity and empathy: Toward racial and educational achievement in the Obama era. *Harvard Educational Review, 79*(2), 278–297.

Harper, S. R. (2009). Niggers no more: A critical race counternarrative on Black male student achievement at predominantly White colleges and universities. *International Journal of Qualitative Studies in Education, 22*(6), 697–712.

Jackson, M. (2017). Covert direction through informal leadership in higher education. In C. Rogers, A. Hilton, & K. Lomotey (Eds.), *Innovative approaches to educational leadership: Selected cases* (pp. 57–72). New York, NY: Peter Lang.

Ladson-Billings, G. (2013). Critical race theory—What it is not! In M. Lynn & A. Dixson (Eds.), *Handbook of critical race theory in education* (pp. 34–47). New York, NY: Routledge.

Leonardo, Z. (2009). *Race, whiteness, and education.* New York, NY: Routledge.

Smith, W. (2010). Toward an understanding of misandric microaggressions and racial battle fatigue among African Americans in historically White institutions. In V. Polite & E. Zamani-Gallaher (Eds.), *The state of the African American male* (pp. 265–277). East Lansing, MI: Michigan State University Press.

Smith, W. A., Allen, W. R., & Danley, L. L. (2007). "Assume the position...you fit the description" psychosocial experiences and racial battle fatigue among African American male college students. *American Behavioral Scientist, 51*(4), 551–578.

Smith, W. A., Hung, M., & Franklin, J. D. (2011). Racial battle fatigue and the miseducation of Black men: Racial microaggressions, societal problems, and environmental stress. *Journal of Negro Education, 80*(1), 63–82.

Smith, W. A., Hung, M., & Franklin, J. D. (2012). Between hope and racial battle fatigue: African American men and race related stress. *Journal of Black Masculinity, 2*(1), 35–58.

Smith, W. A., Yosso, T. J., & Solórzano, D. G. (2006). Challenging racial battle fatigue on historically White campuses: A critical race examination of race-related stress. In C. A. Stanley (Ed.), *Faculty of color teaching in predominantly White colleges and universities* (pp. 299–327). Bolton, MA: Anker.

Solorzano, D., Ceja, M., & Yosso, T. (2000). Critical race theory, racial microaggression, and campus racial climate: The experiences of African American college students. *Journal of Negro Education, 69*(1/2), 60–73.

Stevenson, T. N. (2013). *Racial battle fatigue, role strain, and African-American faculty at public community colleges* (Doctoral dissertation). Retrieved from https://commons.emich.edu/cgi/viewcontent.cgi?referer=https://www.google.com/&httpsredir=1&article=1795&context=theses

Thomas, G. (1981). *Black students in higher education: Conditions and experiences in the 1970s.* Westport, CT: Greenwood Press.

CHAPTER 9

INVISIBLE LIFE IN THE ACADEMY

Experiences of African American Women in Higher Education

Kimberly D. Johnson
The University of Missouri–Kansas City

This chapter explores experiences of African American women staff in higher education. The chapter's focus includes the workplace challenges of African American women staff in higher education; the importance of mentoring and sister circles; the vision of success for support staff; and the coping strategies utilized by African American women to navigate colleague interactions. The recommendations may be used to further discussions regarding how institutions, specifically predominantly White institutions (PWIs), can provide support to African American women staff.

African American women working at colleges and universities across the country face a multitude of issues. For example, Collins (2002) notes that while Black women in academic institutions may differ in their experiences, backgrounds, and beliefs, their struggle to be accepted and respected

No Ways Tired, pages 85–90
Copyright © 2019 by Information Age Publishing

allows them to have a voice in an institution with many views. Reflecting on my experiences as an African American with ten years in Student Affairs, I also discovered that I am not alone in my struggle for visibility. During my dissertation research colleagues from other institutions also shared some of the challenges they face.

According to Collins (1991), Black women's lives are linked to a history of oppression that often allows the devaluation of African American women while encouraging their White counterparts. Scholar Audre Lorde discussed the lived experiences of African American women in society as an insider versus outsider phenomenon and obstacles such as oppression as an intersectional construction in their lives (Collins, 2000). Women of color, particularly Black women, deal with the double jeopardy of being Black and a woman. This duality is a challenge because issues of gender are connected to race and therefore, the two are inseparable.

Women of color often receive limited opportunities to serve in capacities that could offer professional development and access to leadership roles. Bailey (2010) noted that African American female professionals working in higher education experience a lack of support in career advancement, isolation, and discrimination as compared to their White colleagues. As my colleagues, I too experienced obstacles to my career advancement. I witnessed coworkers with less experience and education quickly advance within the institution. However, these obstacles motivated me to succeed.

INVISIBLE VOICE

Maintaining the invisibility of Black women and our ideas has been critical in maintaining social inequalities (Collins, 2000). Not only are Black women voices being silenced, unfortunately, there are some people who deliberately attempt to keep them outside of key conversations. I experienced this when one of my colleagues suggested to our supervisor that I no longer attend leadership team meetings. It quickly became apparent that I was seen as the "help" versus having a true seat at the table. Such actions are common tactics to keep African American women staff invisible.

Using your voice is a strategy to make sure African American women are not left out of the conversation. In an effort to have our voices heard, it is critical that we stay informed of campus projects and initiatives so we can add to the conversation. It is imperative that we use our seat at the table to advocate for others. My supervisor allowed me to be at the table which has allowed me to be informed of top level issues. Even though this experience was a challenge for me, I took advantage of it and sought to understand how institutions work behind the scenes. In the leadership discussions, I become privy to information which allowed me to learn more about the politics and the culture of the institution.

As a woman of color, I have often been in settings on campus where I was the only one of a few persons of color. Some research on African American faculty and staff of color suggests this leads to marginalization (Johnsrud, 1993). Colleagues in my research and others who are African American women staff said they often felt inconspicuous and insignificant in higher education and this feeling became the norm in some workplaces. The discussions also included examples of being excluded because of race, gender, or ranking at the institution. In the end, this exclusion can impact professionals' of color quest to be a full member of the team. Despite these challenges, African American women continue to thrive and succeed despite the obstacles they encounter.

MENTORING MATTERS

As a professional staff member in higher education, it is sometimes difficult to get access to resources that other employees may have in the workplace such as mentors, coaches or advisors to assist you on your journey. Mentoring has been identified as a vital component in career success (Johnsrud, 1993). Mentors, formally or informally, can assist with providing mentee(s) with an opportunity to meet new people, new opportunities, and network with other professionals. Garvey, Stokes, and Megginson (2014) noted the benefits of having a mentor to include the mentee would build self-confidence and willingness to take risks in the workplace; develop independence and maturity in the workplace; and develop the ability to accept criticism and use it for the betterment of their career development. My advancement at the institution was largely in part due to a mentor who gave me opportunities to show my worth, which included serving on committees, training, conference attendance, and opportunities to present. It took another woman of color on campus to provide me with outlets to demonstrate what I could do beyond support staff duties. African American women need an advocate who can speak on their behalf.

Having this mentor made a huge difference in my journey in higher education. This African American administrator who took time to advise me and many others by being a role model and a listening ear when needed. She constantly encouraged me to progress in the workplace by engaging in activities outside of my main duties. I also have a Caucasian mentor who has impacted my educational and professional career journey. Having a mentor and sponsor connected me in ways that not only allowed me visibility on campus, but also allowed me to gain professional development opportunities on campus, in the community, and on a national level.

SISTER CIRCLES

At the core of Black feminist thought is the concept of standpoint, which suggests that the struggle against racism and sexism is a common bond among African American women (Collins, 2002). Consequently, Black women should have an established support network of colleagues both within and outside of their departments (Gregory, 2001), especially those who work on predominantly White campuses. This network will provide someone with whom they can feel safe and share their experiences. These networks can also help guide them through any challenges they face on campus.

African American women in student affairs should identify colleagues who will support them and with whom they have good rapport and similar interests. African American women in higher education who may feel marginalized and isolated need opportunities to share their stories and recount their workplace experiences. To develop this support system, you may have to initiate the connections, but others may initiate connections as well. Listening to the voice of others may assist you with developing your own voice, which will increase your confidence, liberate you, and enhance your visibility on campus. My network helped me stay focused and gave me confidence to stay the course and not give up. It is easier to navigate this world of higher education with support and not on your own.

STRATEGIES FOR SUCCESS: COPING TO SURVIVE

My vision of success for African American women staff is to survive and thrive within the institution no matter what obstacles come their way. In order to succeed within higher education, I offer the following strategies that I have used in my career thus far:

- *Stay informed of university policies.* Learn as much as you can about the institution. Being a well-rounded employee will make you more valuable to the institution. Seek information about the campus overall and understand how your daily work fits into the mission and goals of the institution. This knowledge will not only assist you in your position, but could also possibly lead to other career opportunities within the institution and beyond.
- *Take initiative.* Do not wait for the next assignment. Create opportunities for yourself by suggesting ideas to improve processes. Show that you are interested in becoming knowledgeable about areas beyond your department. This effort will show that you are interested in advancing beyond your current position. If you wait on oppor-

tunities or to be asked to serve, the request may never come. Turn your idea(s) into a project that will help you and the institution.

- *Volunteer.* Serve on committees when the opportunity is presented. This experience will serve you well as it gives others the chance to see what skills you possess. You also will meet other colleagues while working on projects. Find a way to get involved on campus as I have found support staff are often not considered when campus committees are being formed. Also, be sure to connect with the staff association if there is one on campus. Committee work also may give you a chance to lead a team and collaborate with other staff, faculty, and students.
- *Professional resources.* Take advantage of programs offered at your institution as this will assist you with making connections. In talking with other staff, learn about their career paths as these people can be resources as you consider the next step in your career. Engaging in professional development opportunities may assist with dissuading some of the barriers to advancement that African American women face on campus.
- *Seek a mentor.* Mentoring can serve as a beneficial resource for staff who are seeking to build their career (Garvey et al., 2014). African American women benefit from having a mentor to help with guide them in their career and provide insight into strategies to navigate different situations in the workplace.

CONCLUSION

The invisibility that African American women face at institutions of higher education can be combated by moving from an outsider to an insider status. Accordingly, women of color need the tools to navigate this process. Further study about the unique challenges faced by African American women staff is necessary to understand experiences and strategies they employ to resist obstacles related to the underrepresentation, isolation, and marginalization in higher education (Moses, 1989).

REFERENCES

Bailey, K. M. (2010). *The hidden leaves of the baobab tree: Lived experiences of African American female chief academic officers* (Doctoral dissertation). Available from ProQuest Dissertations and Theses database. (UMI No. 3452438)

Collins, P. H. (1991). *Black feminist thought.* New York, NY: Routledge.

Collins, P. H. (2000). *Black feminist thought.* New York, NY: Routledge.

Collins, P. H. (2002). *Black feminist thought: Knowledge, consciousness, and the politics of empowerment.* New York, NY: Routledge.

Garvey, B., Stokes, P., & Megginson, D. (2014). *Coaching and mentoring: Theory and practice.* Thousand Oaks, CA: SAGE.

Gregory, S. T. (2001). Black faculty women in the academy: History, status, and future. In F. B. Bonner & V. G. Thomas (Eds.), Black women in the academy: Challenges and opportunities [Special issue]. *Journal of Negro Education, 70*(3), 124–138.

Johnsrud, L. K. (1993, Spring). Women and minority faculty experiences: Defining and responding to diverse realities. *New Directions for Teaching and Learning, 53,* 3–16.

Moses, Y. (1989). Black women in academe: Issues and strategies. In Benjamin, L. (Ed.), *Black women in the academy: promises and perils* (pp. 23–37). Gainesville: University Press of Florida.

CHAPTER 10

STANDING IN THE GAP

Navigating Othermothering as a Student Affairs Professional

Laila I. McCloud
University of Iowa

Affirming faculty–student interactions have been documented to improve outcomes for students of color on college campuses. These affirming relationships, or specifically othermothering, place additional expectations on Black women student affairs professionals that are often not discussed in graduate preparation programs. This chapter will present an approach to helping Black women student affairs professionals understand and develop ways to engage in healthy forms of othermothering.

I learned early in my professional career the importance of creating and maintaining boundaries with my students. As one of the few (sometimes only) Black professionals on campus, I quickly realized that I would be expected to be all things to everyone, especially Black students. While I wanted to be accessible to my students, I also needed to find ways to protect my time and energy. As a new professional, I made it a practice to not engage with my students on social media or give them my personal cell phone number. It became important to set up these sharp boundaries because I wanted them to see me as a professional. But my methods for managing these boundaries have shifted over time, especially since I became a mother. My students know that while they are a priority, they are not my only priority. However, I am aware that the work of a Black woman in student affairs often extends beyond business hours. In this chapter, I explore how the practice of othermothering influences how I challenge and support college students. Using my own story and the stories of students I have worked with, I provide recommendations for entry and mid-level professionals interested in using othermothering in their practice.

THE STUDENT EXPERIENCE AND OTHERMOTHERING

The first day of my first-year seminar course will be one that I will always remember. Just before the start of class, a White female classmate sat next to me with a slight grin on her face. She leaned over and gently whispered, "This is the closest I've ever been to a Black person." I am sure I gave her a reassuring smile, but I could not push words out of my mouth. This incident occurred in a time before smartphones and social media; otherwise, I might have sarcastically asked her if she wanted to take a photo with me. It was the first time I remember feeling as if my Blackness was on display and that a performance was expected. What I remember most about the aftermath of this incident is that I did not feel like I had an "adult" on campus I could talk to about my experience. My faculty advisor was a White woman, who I liked, but we had not reached that point in our relationship where I felt comfortable processing this experience. Throughout the course of my time at that institution, I would continue to experience microaggressions that I didn't have the emotional maturity to deal with.

Like many first-year college students, I struggled to balance the academic and social expectations of small, private, selective, historically White liberal arts college. It was challenging to come into adulthood in a hostile learning environment while feeling like I did not have the nurturing support of faculty and administrators. There were Black faculty and staff members on campus; however, the assumption that there will be an instant connection between Black students and Black faculty and staff is problematic. As a continuing-generation college student, I did not fit the problematic narrative of an "at-risk" student and was not fully engaged in support systems that might have made my transition a little easier. When I decided to leave the institution the following year, I left determined to find that support system at my new institution.

The experience in my first-year seminar course, along with many other, influence how I interact with students, especially those that hold similar identities. However, it is very important that I do not let my experiences muddy the waters for my students. Their experiences are uniquely their own and it is important that I honor their truth. My identity as a mother has added another layer that influences my relationships with my students and my colleagues. I regularly find myself in a delicate dance between imposed and invited maternal labor, otherwise known as othermothering (Collins, 2002). Othermothering can be understood as going above and beyond the expectations of your role as a student affairs professional. Individuals who engage in othermothering are heavily invested in the emotional, physical, financial, and mental well-being of their students. Research has shown that othermothering is beneficial in increasing the academic success and sense of belonging for Black students (Case, 1997; Guiffrida, 2005; Hirt, Amelink, McFeeters, & Strayhorn, 2008). No one would argue the value of positive relationships between Black students, faculty, and staff. No one would argue the value of positive relationships between Black students, faculty, and staff. In "Beyond the Call of Duty," Flowers, Scott, Riley, and Palmer (2015) assert that othermothering aids in Black student achievement because students have support and access to a "network of care" on campus (p. 68). Yet, much of the literature focuses on the relationships between Black students and Black faculty (Griffin, 2012; Mawhinney, 2011; Tuitt, 2012).

Conversations about the toll maternal labor takes on Black women faculty and staff have been minimal. This type of labor is not included in retention plans or considered in annual performance evaluations. Our students often expect to find comfort and peace when they walk into our offices. How do we manage our desire to engage in intentionally supportive relationships with our students while making sure that our boundaries are clear and healthy?

Expectations for student affairs professionals' work are further complicated by the belief that we should always be available and the ways in which we are expected to support students. Mawhinney (2011) discussed the emotional and physical impact of students' expectations for othermothering:

> The self-sacrificing nature of othermothering often brings in the elements of lack of self-care. Roseboro and Ross (2009) refer to this concept as care-sickness that can often occur with Black women educators when they are just tired from caring too much. I argue that the lack of self-care from care-sickness is fueled by the generation of guilt that occurs among teachers feeling as if they are not providing enough within the teacher–student relational expectations. (p. 217)

Unlike mentoring, othermothering requires a deeper level of care and support for students as they make meaning of their newfound adulthood. When I asked a former student how she understood our relationship, she shared:

> The support is also grounded in true love and wanting the other person to be great and successful. It's different from a mentoring-type relationship. It's more of an intimate relationship. Feelings and emotion-wise. In this type of relationship, I could come to you with anything.

Mothering has also affected my practice because I am intentional about how I use my time and how I communicate my priorities to my students. Now that I am a mother, I think deeply about the type of college experience I want for my child. As a parent, especially during the first year of parenting, it is easy to be consumed by doing everything "right." I think the same is true for emerging student affairs professionals. It is easy to worry about planning the perfect program or always voicing the right words when a student comes to you in distress. I have learned over time that there is no perfect way to parent and there is no perfect way to be a practitioner.

STANDING IN THE GAP

My office is a counterspace against the pervasive racism on historically White college campuses. I can recall numerous occasions where students would walk into my office, close the door, and collapse into a chair. Sometimes they would not mutter a word; they just needed a space where they could breathe or as one student said, "I feel like I am enough here." Other students would say, "We need to talk," and we did. We talked about everything from discovering newfound sexuality to organizing an outline for a paper. I would be lying if I said these conversations came naturally to me. Nonetheless, there were times I felt honored that my students felt comfortable enough to ask me questions and share intimate parts of their life with me. In those instances, I'm reminded of a section from Maya Angelou's book, *Mom & Me & Mom* (2013), where she explores her relationship with her mother,

> . . . I really saw clearly, and for the first time, why a mother is really important. Not just because she feeds and also loves and cuddles and even mollycoddles a child, but because in an interesting and maybe an eerie and unworldly way, she stands in the gap. She stands between the unknown and the known. (p. 170)

When I reflect on my experiences as a practitioner, I think about the ways I have struggled with othermothering. Early in my career, I felt it was important to set boundaries and be taken seriously by my mostly White colleagues. Now that I am a parent and a more seasoned professional, I think less about my White colleagues' expectations and more about my students' needs. I have also come to embrace the fact that othermothering is part of how I show up for my students and colleagues. When someone says to me "You are like our mom," I no longer cringe because it is a source of pride that people know how much I care about them and that my work is important to me.

RECOMMENDATIONS FOR PRACTICE

This section will offer thoughts on how new and mid-level Black women student affairs practitioners can think about how othermothering may influence their practice and their well-being.

Who Is This For?

As I was preparing this chapter, I had a conversation with a friend about how othermothering shows up in my work. In response, she posed the following questions: Is this about you or the students? Are there experiences in your own life that make you feel this is necessary? These are important questions upon which to reflect. As I have previously shared, my own traumatic experiences with whiteness during my undergraduate career definitely shaped my work with students. The majority of my professional career has been at institutions similar to the one I attended. My decision to pursue student affairs as a career was heavily influenced by the lack of support I felt I received as a student. As you engage in othermothering, make reflection an ongoing priority. Make sure that you ask yourself, "Who is this for?" to ensure that you are mindful and not overstepping boundaries, your students' or your own.

A Delicate Dance

One of my favorite lines to share with my students is, "I already have two degrees; my job is to help you get one." I say it so much that before I get the word "degrees" out of my mouth, my students finish the sentence. This statement was not meant to hold my education over their head; it was an attempt to let them know that I have some understanding of the journey they were on. More importantly, it was my way of communicating to them the nature of our relationship. My students knew they would receive support from me, but they would be held accountable for their actions. The delicate dance between cheerleader and conduct officer was initially difficult for me to manage. Over time, it became second nature and students knew that even in difficult times, they could come to me and we would figure out the best course of action. As you engage in othermothering, think about the ways you both challenge and support your students. It is important to maintain a healthy balance of the two for a healthy relationship.

Everything to Everyone

There is an assumption that the mere presence of a Black faculty or staff member will increase the sense of belonging among Black students. There is also an assumption that all Black student affairs professionals have an innate ability to connect with Black students. In contrast, there is an assumption that Black professionals will be unable to authentically connect with students who do not identify as Black. This narrative is dangerous and perpetuates White supremacy. During the course of my career, I have had to remind colleagues I cannot be all things to every student. While othermothering is a part of who I am, not every student I interact with welcomes or needs that. As you engage in othermothering, recognize that every student may not respond to this way of being. It is not possible to be all things to all students, but your students will know that you care by your actions.

Check In

It has always been important for me to check in with my students about how they experience our relationship. As with any relationship, checking in is important to make sure that everyone involved feels supported and respected. Check-ins are not only a way to help with the care sickness as noted by Mawhinney (2011), but also a way to model self-care and boundary setting for students. I remember sitting down for a monthly one-on-one with a student who was preparing for a semester of difficult classes. We began our conversation with me asking him, "What do you need from me this semester?" Often, students are stumped because it is the first time they have heard this type of query. As you engage in other mothering, it is helpful to have students identify their needs and develop the language to articulate them. As your students share what they need, respond with what you can and cannot do, which can also be a good time to connect your students with additional resources that will help them on their journey.

CONCLUSION

Othermothering is a valuable way of being for Black women student affairs practitioners. However, it requires ongoing reflection and boundary setting to ensure that it does not lead to unhealthy relationships or deficient well-being for those involved. It is notable that we often stand in the gap between the known and unknown about the realities of being Black on a college campus.

REFERENCES

Angelou, M. (2013). *Mom & me & mom.* New York, NY: Random House.

Case, K. I. (1997). African American othermothering in the urban elementary school. *The Urban Review, 29*(1), 25–39.

Collins, P. H. (2002). *Black feminist thought: Knowledge, consciousness, and the politics of empowerment.* New York, NY: Routledge.

Flowers, A. M., Scott, J. A., Riley, J. R., & Palmer, R. T. (2015). Beyond the call of duty: Building on other mothering for improving outcomes at historically Black colleges and universities. *Journal of African American Males in Education, 6*(1), 59–73.

Guiffrida, D. (2005). Othermothering as a framework for understanding African American students' definitions of student-centered faculty. *The Journal of Higher Education, 76*(6), 701–723.

Griffin, K. A. (2012). Black professors managing mentorship: Implications of applying social exchange frameworks to our understanding of the influence of student interaction on scholarly productivity. *Teachers College Record, 114*(5), 1–37.

Hirt, J. B., Amelink, C. T., McFeeters, B. B., & Strayhorn, T. L. (2008). A system of othermothering: Student affairs administrators' perceptions of relationships with students at Historically Black Colleges. *NASPA Journal, 45*(2), 210–236.

Mawhinney, L. (2011). Othermothering: A personal narrative exploring relationships between Black female faculty and students. *Negro Educational Review, 62*(1–4), 213

Tuitt, F. (2012). Black like me: Graduate students' perceptions of their pedagogical experiences in classes taught by Black faculty in a predominantly White institution. *Journal of Black Studies, 43*(2), 186–206.

CHAPTER 11

BROKEN BUT WHOLE

How Difficult Transitions Add Value for African American New Professionals in Student Affairs

Sharee L. Myricks
Indiana University–Purdue University Indianapolis
& Ivy Tech Community College, Indianapolis

This chapter provides a personal narrative regarding difficult personal and professional experiences within the career of an African American new professional in student affairs. The chapter features reflections on placing a positive value on adverse experiences to further one's professional and personal development. A theoretical framework of adult transitional theory is briefly applied to action strategies to assist other African American new professionals in student affairs with navigating difficult life transitions. Overall, the chapter provides a perspective for new African American professional colleagues to consider on their career journey when encountering difficult transitions, a topic scholarship commonly overlooks in student affairs conversations.

No Ways Tired, pages 99–107
Copyright © 2019 by Information Age Publishing
All rights of reproduction in any form reserved.

Within this book, the editors encouraged authors to share personal narratives higher education shies away from—the truth about experiences people of color face in the field. I desire to go further. It is important to provide guidance to our emerging colleagues about career transitions as well as personal life experiences such as getting married, welcoming a child, or exploring a new state/city via relocation for a job (Myricks, 2017). There also should be a balance where we share rough transitions encountered in addition to the positive events, especially the unique stories experienced by African American professionals in our field.

Student affairs is viewed as a "warm and fuzzy" profession, one that is constantly inclusive and diverse. Literature written in the field, such as *Beginning Your Journey: A Guide for New Professionals in Student Affairs* by Amey and Reesor (2015), enforces this perception despite the daily racial difficulties African American professionals face both on campus and within our society, impacting our professional practice in higher education. African American new professionals serving college students, while immersed in campus academic and social spaces, are working despite finding themselves broken from racial battle fatigue or personal stressors (Smith, Yosso, & Solórzano, 2011). I believe we can bring our whole selves to our work when we are broken, especially when we are passionate about what we do.

By sharing difficult transitions we face as African American students affairs administrators, African American new professionals can learn to navigate situations with practical insight, discover coping strategies, and become inspired to successfully face adversity. Experienced African American student affairs professionals should challenge themselves to become vulnerable, disclosing stories of confronting personal and professional difficulty in which they learned valuable, practical lessons in their careers. As a result, this effort can aid in the growth of new African American student affairs professionals who encounter difficult events and transitions in their careers. For instance, I will share personal narratives of two difficult transitions I experienced as an African American student affairs new professional—an office crisis involving a colleague of color and the impact of my divorce. My hope is to not only provide insight on how I faced difficult transitions within my career, but also the reflective perspective on how such experiences can add value to the careers of African American new professionals in student affairs.

DIFFICULT TRANSITIONS AT THE WORKPLACE

Coping with a crisis that occurs in one's department/office can be personal in nature and hard to endure. There is no case study that will prepare you for a real incident. For example, the former director of my office, a young man of color, faced adversity when he was publicly accused of sexual assault. He had quickly become an assistant dean of students, earned a doctorate degree, and was considered an emerging leader in student conduct practice. He was placed in a situation none of his colleagues knew how to get him out of, if it was possible. Many who worked with him regularly were unsure if he would professionally survive it. It was hurtful to witness his career being halted by a single accusation. Personally, the situation felt like a conspiracy to bring "the man of color" down, even with the accuser being a woman of color.

As an African American professional woman, I felt that I could not talk about my perspective in the office, to other colleagues within the student affairs division, or within the institution overall. I sensed my views would be taken under the "angry Black woman" prism—a woman of color saying the man of color in the office was wrongly accused due to his race, blinded by the reality of the total situation. However, I did indeed believe my former director was experiencing professional injustice due to his race. I know now that my frustration and despair were valid emotions.

As the situation played on, the university decided to cut ties with my former director, despite the fact there were two formal external investigations that concluded my colleague was not guilty. My perception of being unsafe amongst my colleagues increased as gossip within the student affairs division suggested that my colleague's vices got him into the situation. Even though he was falsely accused and proven innocent, White colleagues who had once considered my former director as a professional darling now tore him down. For the first time in my career, I believed that no matter the level of education obtained or the amount of experience acquired by a professional in the field, even in the supposedly liberal and accepting field of student affairs, one isolated incident could hold back or end a career of a professional of color. As a result, a sense of hopelessness in my professional outlook bled into my work as I grieved for my former colleague and considered my future in the field.

However, this feeling would be short-lived. Prior to any knowledge of this crisis, I had made the decision to seek opportunities to depart from the institution. Quickly upon accepting a position at an institution where I felt safe to share my opinions, I joined the Black Faculty and Staff Council for the first time in my career. My goal in becoming a member of the council was to find academic and social spaces on campus where African American professionals are supporting each other during their tenure at the institution. I would also fellowship with seasoned African American colleagues whom I could go to with my frustrations and emotions regarding the systematic mistreatment of coworkers of colors should they arise.

PERSONAL DIFFICULT TRANSITIONS' IMPACT
ON PROFESSIONAL PERFORMANCE

Difficult transitions in an individual's career can also stem from challenges in their personal lives. For example, within eight months of the aforementioned office crisis, I filed for divorce. The death of a significant relationship is never easy and the end of a marriage typically comprises legal, economic, and parental ramifications that would definitely drain the energy out of anyone. Unlike the crisis situation, during the difficult transition and continuous adjustment of enduring a divorce, I found myself spending a lot of time trying to hide my emotions throughout the workday. I could not quite manage the sentimentalities that ran through my mind all day, especially if I was alone at my desk. I would find myself crying at my workspace or losing focus as I worked on projects. Before meetings, my anxiety would rise as I would become self-conscious about informing colleagues of the reason behind my name change. I was definitely broken, but I gave all I had left to serve students with a positive spirit.

It was only a matter of time before I declined emotionally due to my lack of self-care. In the beginning, I would become easily overwhelmed by the constant stress of the divorce, the effort to do my student affairs role well, and the management of personal obligations. Often, I would experience a heavy weariness of my body and could not think straight. This feeling of physical distress was only alleviated by going home early from work, having a (large) glass of wine, and heading to sleep. I kept this routine to myself. I told myself this pattern of events would expire in due time.

However, on a sunny morning about five months into the divorcing process, I became so overwhelmed during a presentation I experienced tightness in my shoulders, shortness of breath, intense moments of paranoia, and the inability to think straight or talk in complete sentences. I was having an anxiety attack. I decided to leave the event early and proceeded with my routine; but first called my best friend to reduce my anxiety. After explaining the above events, she asked me to seek professional help. Interestingly, student affairs masters' programs have a foundation in a counseling practice approach and I had referred students to the counseling center—even sometimes walking a few over to put them at ease—yet, in practicing self-care to maintain a work–life balance, seeking professional psychological or mental health care was my last resort. The following week, I started my free therapy sessions with my employee assistance service program provided within my institution's benefits package.

THE VALUE IN DIFFICULTY—REFLECTION
AND ACTION STRATEGIES

The narratives regarding experiences with a difficult transition, such as the two revealed within this chapter, can be framed by Schlossberg's (1981) research, "Analyzing Human Adaptation to Transition," also known as "Transition Theory." While introduced to student affairs professionals as a means to offer insight on understanding the phenomenon of college student transition, Schlossberg's theory also focuses on adult transition. When applied to the practice of navigating difficult personal and professional transitions, a transition theory can offer perspective and strategies to assist African American new professionals to find value within their challenges as well as adjust successfully to their careers. Schlossberg's (1981, 1984) transition theory provides insight into the characteristics of the transition and characteristics of the individual at various levels of adversity experienced during adult transition. The research focused on understanding and assisting adults with life change which were anticipated, unanticipated life change, and events which did not occur but were expected. Schlossberg, Waters, and Goodman (1995) expanded Schlossberg's initial research by examining common variables that produce a positive outcome of adaption within the adult transition process, which includes role change, affect, source, timing, onset, and duration. As African American new professionals apply adult transition theory into the practice of their own self-care, they can develop coping skill sets that could be applicable to other situations of hardship during their careers.

Holder and Vaux's (1998) perception regarding African American professionals encountering occupational stress and crisis is also important during the adult transition of African American new professionals in student affairs. Their research found that racial/ethnic professionals encounter various workplace experiences focused on race-related stressors, race-related climate, workplace racial treatment, and personal discrimination—all indirect issues associated with the crisis narrative shared in this chapter.

African American new professionals need tools in their skillset to navigate race-related incidents in higher education and the larger society, which will impact their practice. Unfortunately, student affairs master's programs do not necessarily equip African American new professionals with preparation for encountering institutional marginalization. Nevertheless, I leaned heavily on professional networking with seasoned African American professionals in student affairs who were important in my career, especially during a crisis. Our profession stresses the impact of cultivating the mentor and colleague relationship and accordingly, I advise African American new professionals in student affairs to make these mentoring relationships rich, regular, and relevant. I utilized my mentors to assist me in navigating my feelings and actions during a crisis with countless discussions regarding how they dealt with a race-related climate, workplace racial treatment, and personal discrimination. The exchange of dialogue was safe and provided me with a sense of security to be confident in my observations of the situation. In addition, due to the type of mentoring relationship established, the seasoned African African professionals allowed me to openly process my experience; I correspondingly enabled the mentors to provide critical feedback or insightful perceptions and clear any misinterpretations I held.

RECOMMENDATIONS FOR NEW PROFESSIONALS

African American new professionals in student affairs must also expand their understanding of the mentoring relationship in our field to fully become successful in developing resiliency regarding racial discrimination in our field. I strongly advise African American new professionals to not only develop a circle of mentors for the networking opportunities (i.e., job referrals, career advancement), but to also gain resources that will assist in the coping process.. Upon reflection of my crises, I found that having real social capital involves being involved in relationships to help you and others function effectively. Translated, I may be broken, but I have my supportive colleagues and mentors who assist me to be whole (Myricks, 2017). The true power of rich, regular, and relevant mentoring from African American seasoned professionals during my crisis included the exchange of knowledge, yielding a *positive effect* of transitioning to my new workplace and institution. I was able to release the sense of hopelessness I felt as a result of incidents.

Snowden (2001) and Powell, Adams, Cole-Lewis, Agyemang, and Upton (2016) are insightful regarding African Americans attitudes towards mental health. Snowden (2001) asserts, "Many African Americans suffer from mental health problems and would benefit from timely access to appropriate forms of [professional] care. However, few seek treatment from outpatient providers in the specialty mental health sector..." (p. 181). When encountering a difficult transition, African American professionals prefer coping resources such as turning to friends and family, consulting with religious figure(s), and/or "doing something" to resolve the issue (Snowden, 2001). Consequently, I believe African American new professionals should develop a self-care plan that includes regular professional therapy early on within their careers.

During my divorce, I waited before seeking professional help, despite the various signs of emotional hardship. From the knowledge gained through my formal training and practical wisdom within student affairs, I was aware that I was not coping with the situation well. Variable *timing* (Schlossberg et al., 1995) also suggests an awareness of when one's acts in response to an issue has bearing on the positive impact of the transition. It is my belief, supported by Snowden's (2001) research, had I sought professional mental health services sooner, I could have avoided my emotional distress escalating to an unbearable physical incident (i.e., panic attack). Not only is *timely* access to counseling service important, but emotional and psychological difficulties could be subsided at a cost-effective and trial basis by utilizing the employee assistance program. These efforts could initiate gradual *onset* by developing a mental health support system while promoting the African American new professionals' psychosocial competence by exploring revised or new coping techniques with a mental health professional. After visiting with a counselor for five sessions, I was able to establish better coping skills, work through personal errors when addressing relationship issues, and receive validation on reflections of events that led to my divorce. I believe that African American new professionals who seek professional therapy will become more confident about their coping plans as well as receptive to seeking regular mental health services.

Another reflective lesson was insight into the life-long cycle of "parenting." African American new professionals might look to their parental figures for advice on navigating difficult transitions. Likewise, I employed my mother and father to "parent me" even as an early thirty-year-old. Through my divorce, I was quite surprised at their willingness and vulnerability in sharing their narratives as divorcees. It is advised that African American new professionals be humble enough to allow one's parental figures to "parent" them, as I found my parents had life experiences from which I could learn. More importantly, engaging regularly about my difficult transition made me feel whole, especially more so when I felt broken.

Lastly, in regard to the work we do in student affairs, African American new professionals can apply reflective lessons to our interaction with students and their parents to improve our practice (Myricks, 2017). Often, I conduct academic advising meetings in which both the parent and student attend. One's formal training considers the parent's attendance as an extension of the student's support system; others would consider the situation as a parent not enabling their child to become a leader in their educational pursuits. Yet, until my divorce occurred, I rarely reflected on the matters that mother, father, or loved ones may be "parenting" their student through. Maybe the student is encountering a difficult transition, just like yourself. With the increase of students with mental health issues and disabilities as well as the use of opioid drug abuse, it is not unlikely to interact with students who might be going through or coming out of a very difficult situation. While we may quickly judge the parent for being overly involved, we should also consider the "lifelong parenting" concept as we never know what is going on in someone's personal lives.

CONCLUSION

African American new professionals can bring their whole selves to the practice of student affairs, even when they are broken. When one is passionate about what we do, our work interconnects with our purpose, bringing a sense of hopefulness regarding our existence in the profession and the world (Myricks, 2017). However, it is vital for African Americans new professionals to develop coping skills and utilize all resources at their disposal to successful navigate through difficult personal and professional transitions. Optimistically, action strategies guided by an adult transition theoretical framework can aid African American new professionals with tangible approaches to decrease the likelihood of experiencing a "deficit situation" within the adaption process during transitions—an unstable transitional state within the new environment or status (Schlossberg, 1981). As a result, African American new professionals can be retained in the field of student affairs and build both personal as well as professional resilience.

REFERENCES

Amey, M. J., & Reesor, L. M. (2015). *Beginning your journey: A guide for new professionals in student affairs* (4th ed.). Washington, DC: National Association for Student Affairs Administrators in Higher Education.

Holder, J. C., & Vaux, A. (1998). African American professionals: Coping with occupational stress in predominantly White work environments. *Journal of Vocational Behavior, 53*(3), 315–333. https://doi.org/10.1006/jvbe.1998.1640

Myricks, S. L. (2017). *Broken but whole: Difficult transitions #addvalue as a new professional and graduate students.* [Web log post]. Retrieved from https://www.naspa.org/constituent-groups/posts/broken-but-whole-difficult-transitions-addvalue-as-a-new-professional-grad

Powell, W., Adams, L. B., Cole-Lewis, Y., Agyemang, A., & Upton, R. D. (2016). Masculinity and race-related factors as barriers to health help-seeking among African American men. *Behavioral Medicine, 42*(3), 150–163. https://doi.org/10.1080/08964289.2016.1165174

Schlossberg, N. K. (1981). A model for analyzing human adaptation. *The Counseling Psychologist, 9*(2), 2–18. https://doi.org/10.1177/001100008100900202

Schlossberg, N. K. (1984). *Counseling adults in transition.* New York, NY: Springer.

Schlossberg, N. K., Waters, E. B., & Goodman, J. (1995). *Counseling adults in transition* (2nd ed.). New York, NY: Springer.

Smith, W. A., Yosso, T. J., & Solórzano, D. G. (2011). Challenging racial battle fatigue on historically White campuses: A critical race examination of race-related stress. In J. Morrison & R. D. Coates (Eds.), *Covert racism theories, institutions, and experiences, 32,* 211–238. https://doi.org/10.1163/ej.9789004203655.i-461.82

Snowden, L. R. (2001). Barriers to effective mental health services for African Americans. *Mental Health Services Research, 3*(4), 181–187. https://doi .org/10.1023/A:1013172913880

CHAPTER 12

BALANCING SELF-PRESENTATION AND AUTHENTIC LEADERSHIP THROUGH MIDDLE MANAGEMENT

Uzoma F. Obidike
Indiana State University

Navigating middle management in student affairs came with a number of experiences that have shaped the professional I am today. Some of these experiences were challenges and others were just moments in my career trajectory that taught me valuable lessons. In this chapter, I will share my experiences with navigating self-identity in the workplace, insecurities, and self-doubt when transitioning to the next-level, balancing middle management, and dealing with the loss of my job. The primary constant in each experience was how I strategically handled each one by balancing authenticity with impression management. As I share about each experience, I will also include the lessons I learned along the way.

No Ways Tired, pages 109–117
Copyright © 2019 by Information Age Publishing
All rights of reproduction in any form reserved.

Being born in America to two Nigerian parents, I have had to deal with issues relating to racial and ethnic identity all of my life, including in the workplace. Having lived in both countries, I never felt fully American nor did I ever feel fully Nigerian. My identity encompasses both nationalities. Most of the time, whenever I talked about my heritage at work with my colleagues, it was usually in a lighthearted or educational manner. My peers always seemed fascinated by my life experiences that I shared with them. However, in certain scenarios when I felt the pressure to pick between agreeing with the perspectives of Black people and those of White people, my identity and loyalty were questioned.

IDENTITY IN THE WORKPLACE

In America, there is a paradigm that says all racial issues either need to fall into the Black or the White category; this is referred to as the Black–White binary (Delgado & Stefancic, 2012). Delgado and Stefancic wrote that this belief has always been present in American society, therefore it continues to be perpetuated. They also posited that each person has more than one identity, and this is true for me. Whenever there was a racial tension at the institution, I felt pressure from my Black American colleagues to take their side. If I did not, then some of those individuals would say that I was taking the side of White people. Delgado and Stefancic noted that at times, people who do not fit the binary feel as though their identity does not exist. Often, I felt as though my Nigerian American perspective did not matter or count.

Binary thinking is a way for the predominant society to place individuals of different minoritized groups against each other (Delgado & Stefancic, 2012). Some of my Black American peers would tell me, "You look Black, therefore White people will always see you as Black." I will never deny my race; however, my Nigerian American experience and that of the Black American experience are simply not the same. If I tried to explain the differences to some of my Black American peers at work, sharing these distinctions would at times cause some conflict. The conversation always led to "Is it true that Africans don't like Black people?" or "Why do Africans always think they are better than us?" One time, my department was in the process of being restructured. To my recollection, I was the only Black person promoted into a new role. Though I did not have a full-time staff report to me, the role was a step up from entry-level. The only space available for me so happened to be in the student affairs suite where the offices of the senior administration staff were located. I was the only Black person in the suite. I remember one of my Black American peers jokingly telling me that I was a "house nigger," and essentially, the token Black person in the in-crowd because I made it to the proverbial ivory tower. Though I considered the statement very divisive, I shrugged it off that day because I was tired of having the same conversations about race when I did not feel it was warranted. According to Massé, Miller, Kerr, and Ortiz (2007), sometimes immigrants feel the need to assimilate into the culture, while still maintaining their identity. Though I am a daughter of immigrant parents, I have often had to assimilate during my career. Often at student affairs meetings, and programs with students, we engaged in conversations on diversity and inclusion. Therefore, on occasion, I had to choose the side of the Black binary because that was my only option. At times, I had to strategically balance the display of my true identities in order to avoid controversy.

THE IMPOSTOR SYNDROME

At my next institution, I did not deal with a lot of the race and ethnic identity issues as I had previously. In this new role, I was charged to lead a much larger office and I had to supervise a full-time staff. During this time, I experienced what is known as the impostor phenomenon or more commonly known as the impostor syndrome. This psychological experience occurs when a person feels that they do not deserve their accomplishments and, in some ways, also feels like a fraud for somehow managing to achieve their level of success (Clance, 1985). I definitely felt this way at first when I assumed this new responsibility because not only did I have to manage a full-time staff, I also had to oversee my office for multiple campus locations. At the time, I was in my late 20s and I was younger than all of the people who reported to me. Needless to say, I was unsure that I was truly ready for what was to come. Though I had met all of the academic and job experience requirements, for some reason I felt like there may have been a mistake with me being hired. I felt the fear and anxiety creep in when I sat in on my first leadership team meeting. Many of the team members in this group had been at the institution for over 20 years. I looked around and thought, "What am I doing here?" I had only been out of graduate school for 4 years and I remember attaining the coveted director title much quicker than most of my graduate school cohort peers. I knew this fact to be true because social media kept me abreast of their professional statuses. Though I was proud of my accomplishments, there were a lot of times I felt unsure. It must have been a mistake that the selection committee chose me for this position. Maybe I was not ready for this new role because I felt it was too soon. I had fears that I would be judged for being young or that I would not be able to fulfill my new responsibilities.

Whether I believed that I could do the job, or if I deserved to be there, I was indeed hired to do the work. Therefore, doing the work is exactly what I did. The one thing that was important for me was not to let others see what

I was feeling nor did I share my insecurities and doubts with anyone at the office. I did not want to tell anyone I needed help, so I would use Google to search topics like "how to manage a full-time staff" or "what leadership style should I use as a new manager?" Graduate school taught me how to thrive in entry level student affairs jobs, but I never had training on middle-management. I wanted to be perceived as a credible and competent leader; therefore, I did all that I could to get in the right mindset so that I could do the work confidently. I needed to believe that I could actually do the work. When a person believes they can accomplish goals in certain situations, this is what Bandura (1995) referred to as self-efficacy.

To move toward my goal of doing the work effectively, I took my time to observe and familiarize myself with the campus culture. In addition, I met one-on-one with each member of my team to get an understanding of how things operated prior to my arrival. Early in this role, my priority was to build genuine relationships with my team and other colleagues at the institution. Other strategies that helped me feel more confident in my role were speaking up at meetings and taking on projects or committee roles that further gave me credibility. I was really great at building genuine relationships with colleagues in various departments and at the other campus locations. In turn, I was able to organically secure mentors and attract sponsors who helped me along my career trajectory at the institution.

The impostor phenomenon crept up at other points in my career, but I realized it only occurred when I was met with a new or daunting challenge. Examples of these feelings of being a fraud were when my supervisor asked me to take on additional campuses while overseeing additional staff and also when I began my doctoral journey. In both of these instances, I felt insecure about my knowledge and expertise. Therefore, I made myself believe that I was not capable of doing the work. I am not a quitter, so I pushed through and persevered in both situations. I have since come to accept that insecurities and self-doubt will always be present when I take on new opportunities that will advance me to the next level. Also, being aware of these feelings, and knowing how to manage my emotions with grace at work, have always helped me to endure nonetheless.

LEADING FROM THE MIDDLE

Managing from the middle was one of the toughest challenges I have experienced in my career. Being a middle manager required me to be politically savvy and to have a strong and supportive network in the workplace. In addition, being a good middle manager required resilience and influence, while having to balance leading others and having to be led (Taylor, 2007).

What added to the complexity of the situation was that I worked at a large institution with multiple campus locations.

I learned a lot about organizational politics while in this role. Middle management comes with having to understand the politics, build alliances with individuals of influence, and manage conflict between upper management and frontline staff (Bolman & Deal, 2013). Working at a multi-campus institution, there were so many levels of reporting that required multiple lines of communication. It was not uncommon for members of my team to feel uncomfortable when they received direction from someone in senior-level management. Then, I have been in situations where some officials at the top wanted me to manage my staff in a manner that best suited their needs. In terms of information sharing, there were also times when I had to keep confidential information from my team members that could have potentially had an impact on their roles. Withholding certain information from my team members was difficult for me because I had built such a strong trust with them, so I felt disloyal for not being able to keep them informed. On the other hand, there were times when members of my team would share information they asked me to keep from my supervisors. Needless to say, I was figuratively stuck in the middle during my time in middle-management. Decision-making for me came with a lot of risk because I had to advocate for my team while also ensuring my supervisors knew that I was committed to their vision.

Building and maintaining a strong team is dependent on its leader. Credibility is very important for a leader when seeking followership (Kouzes & Posner, 2011). I needed my team to be able to trust me and share in the same vision that I had for our office. I did this by both inspiring hope in my team and by having strong moral beliefs. As a leader, Kouzes and Posner (2011) revealed that you can build and maintain credibility by inspiring hope in constituents. They wrote that leaders are able to remain credible when they can help to uplift the spirits of other people and give them a renewed confidence in what the future will bring. During my years as a mid-level manager, I had to instill a level of hope for my team, even when things at the top seemed uncertain. I also needed to be credible for my supervisors. In addition to hope, it was important for me as a mid-level manager to also embody strong moral beliefs. According to Northouse (2013), having strong moral beliefs, being consistent, and having compassion are all important in authentic leadership. He also wrote that having genuine qualities through actions were essential. Being open and honest definitely helped keep communications lines open between me and my team as well as between me and my supervisors.

There is a lot of strategy involved when navigating organizations (Bolman & Deal, 2013). Strategy is especially key when building and maintaining relationships. In working closely with so many individuals at the institution, I had to learn when and when not to speak and how to work with different personalities. I also had to identify whom to trust and whom not to trust. I had to do all of this while putting on the best professional persona that I knew possible. Remaining authentic to myself was always something I strived to do while navigating the political system. Being myself in this system was a struggle; nevertheless, I certainly put forth the effort.

DEALING WITH THE UNEXPECTED JOB LOSS

I never expected the day would come when my job would be eliminated. However, it happened to me and I had no choice but to deal with the consequences. During this time, there was a lot of change going on within the institution. Change in organizations can cause structural and political barriers like loss of clarity, stability, and influence (Bolman & Deal, 2013). Bolman and Deal also noted that there can be an increase in friction between those with higher power and those of lesser power. I experienced the aforementioned political barriers when my organization experienced massive change. Though I was soon to be out of a job and things at work seemed to be falling apart for many of the employees, I made sure to keep my composure and bow out gracefully with dignity.

The institution was undergoing a financial crisis and therefore, had to resort to a reduction in force. I remember the day when one of the decision makers, a White woman, called me into the human resources office to deliver the news. She seemed very surprised at my composure and told me that I was "handling it very well." I told her that I was sure that she, and the other committee members, had very difficult decisions to make and I did not take it personally. In the back of my mind, I wondered how she expected me to handle the news. Was that a microaggression? Did she expect me to start cursing or wailing hysterically? She has known me for years and should have known my professional character. Ultimately, I smiled at her and the other two people in the room and told them I was grateful for the time I was able to serve at the institution. I also wished them well since they had to make this announcement to many more unsuspecting employees. As the days went on, I could not help but question why *my* position was eliminated. Was it due to something I did or something I said? Was it because of my race or was it political? Due to the variety of experiences I encountered during the organizational change, I had so many questions.

In addition to my questions, there were also a lot of rumors and speculations circulating around the office space regarding why and how the decisions were made. After listening to all the gossip, I determined to myself that I would not feed into all of the noise. It was already a stressful time for me and I did not have the mental energy to deal with the workplace drama.

I was planning my wedding, preparing for my in-laws to visit the country, and writing my dissertation. I decided there were so many more important things to worry about than to be concerned about why my position was cut. At that point in time, it clearly did not matter. The decision was already made, and I had about four weeks to plan for my next steps. Knowing that my time at the institution was soon ending, it was disheartening because not only was I losing my income and benefits, I was also losing a team and a role I had loved which was the hardest part about the change.

When dealing with change, Bolman and Deal (2013) recommended putting together a strategy that includes bringing the team together and keeping them uplifted during tumultuous times. They also recommend that leaders should empower their team to move forward and stay focused on their work. I did all of these things, including leaving a succession plan for the team. I waited until my last week to start gathering my belongings because I wanted to be sure that I remained present, physically and mentally, until my last day. Although my mind was filled with frustration and disappointment about the committee's decision and the uncertainties about my future, I was determined that I would not allow my team, peers, or supervisors to see me down and to carry myself in a respectable manner. In my opinion, the workplace was simply not the place to show my true emotions. Many of my peers, who also suffered the same fate, used up the remaining of their sick time and took off work. There were definitely days I wanted to do the same; however, I did not have it in me to let my team down. I was their leader until the very end. I also did not want to appear as though the loss had that much impact on me because that could have caused a trickle-down effect to my team.

During my final weeks at the institution, I was strategically planning for my next move. Just before my departure, I had quickly made it to two final round interviews at other institutions of higher education. I received one offer, but later turned it down because it was not the best fit and a few months later, I accepted a new position that I held for a year. The role was not at an institution of higher education; however, it fit well with my career interests and personal values. During that time, I began an adjunct teaching role at the collegiate level. I also decided to take a break from full-time employment to focus on personal endeavors, including to finish my dissertation. Only time will tell if this is the end of my career journey in student affairs or if this is just a pause along the way.

FINAL THOUGHTS AND WORDS OF ADVICE

In a process known as impression management, Goffman (1959) wrote that people, subconsciously or intentionally, present themselves in a way that will influence the perceptions of other people. During most of the experiences I shared in this chapter, I was not aware that I was practicing impression management. However, after much reflection, I can see clearly that having a strategic combination of authenticity and self-presentation allowed me to be a stronger, successful leader over the years. I recommend that student affairs professionals utilize a similar balanced approach when navigating their careers. In this conclusion, I offer my recommendations for each of my experiences shared in this chapter.

In the student affairs profession, administrators spend a lot of time focusing on the identity development of students. However, it is extremely important for us to remember that our own identity as post-graduates, and professionals, are also relevant. Do not feel pressured to fit into an identity box that someone else has created for you. Do not be ashamed to express your true self at work. Lastly, it is important to understand that not everyone is going to agree with your diverse perspectives and points of view, and that is okay. In fact, as you develop your leadership skills, being able to have your own unique voice and stand by your words will take you far in this work.

The further along I go in my career, the more I have heard from colleagues that they too have experienced, and continue to experience, the impostor phenomenon. Fear or insecurities should not stop you from reaching your career goals. On the contrary, these are the feelings that are needed to fuel you to keep going and thrive in your career. So many people do not succeed because they have allowed fear and self-doubt hold them back. I know that if I let fear, insecurities, and uncertainty discourage me, I may never have taken on the roles and opportunities that were presented to me.

As I take a closer look at the experiences that shaped who I am as a professional today, I recognize that I needed to have a strong balance of being true to my personal values and beliefs and being able to manage my feelings and emotions in the workplace. From my perspective, managing your emotions in the workplace is key. It is necessary to practice discernment when deciding how to react to certain situations and certain people. Before you decide to react, consider the consequences your response will have on you and those involved. There will be times when you will need to have a voice and take a stance on an issue. Then there will be times when you will need to put aside your ego and let it go. Overall, knowing how to navigate organizational politics is very necessary.

Lastly, diversify your experience and build a strong, and extensive, network early in your career so that you can be more marketable when you are ready—or forced—to advance. Moving up in student affairs may require you to a move to another geographic area. Note that the higher up you go, there will be fewer positions available to you. Other options include staying in the area but accepting a lower ranking title or a lower salary. You may even have to consider leaving the field. By being clear on your long-term professional goals and having a career advancement plan, with alternative career paths, you will be better prepared when it is time to move on to your next role.

REFERENCES

Bandura, A. (Ed.). (1995). *Self-efficacy in changing societies.* Cambridge, England: Cambridge University Press.

Bolman, L. G., & Deal, T. E. (2013). *Reframing organizations: Artistry, choice, and leadership* (5th ed.). San Francisco, CA: Jossey-Bass.

Clance, P. R. (1985). *The impostor phenomenon: Overcoming the fear that haunts your success.* Atlanta, GA: Peachtree.

Delgado, R., & Stefancic, J. (2012). *Critical race theory: An introduction* (2nd ed.). New York: New York University Press.

Goffman, E. (1959). *The presentation of self in everyday life.* New York, NY: Doubleday.

Kouzes, J. M., & Posner, B. Z. (2011). *Credibility: How leaders gain and lose it, why people demand it,* (2nd ed.). San Francisco, CA: Jossey-Bass.

Massé, J., Miller, E., Kerr, K., & Ortiz, A. M. (2007). Negotiating middle ground: The experiences of midmanagers of color in student affairs. In R. L. Ackerman & L. D. Roper, *The mid-level manager in student affairs* (pp. 155–176). Washington, DC: National Association of Student Personnel Administrators.

Northouse, P. G. (2013). *Leadership: Theory and practice,* (6th ed.). Thousand Oaks, CA: SAGE.

Taylor, C. M. (2007). Leading from the middle. In R. L. Ackerman & L. D. Roper, *The mid-level manager in student affairs* (pp. 127–153). Washington, DC: National Association of Student Personnel Administrators.

CHAPTER 13

CLAIMING VOICE, CLAIMING SPACE

Using a Liberatory Praxis Towards Thriving as Student Affairs Professionals of Color

Roberto C. Orozco
Rutgers University

DanaMichelle Harris
Rutgers University

Tennille Haynes
Rutgers University

Cynthia N. Sánchez Gómez
Rutgers University

Merylou Rodriguez
Rutgers University

No Ways Tired, pages 119–129

In this chapter, we interrogate the questioning of spaces we are permitted to claim. We ask ourselves, "What does it mean to thrive in student affairs and higher education?" and "How do we individually and collectively engage in a liberatory praxis?" We provide an overview of how we define what it means to claim voice, claim space, and thrive within multiple contexts. As we share our *testimonios* (narratives), we will incorporate sociopolitical histories to re-center a story of marginalization as a way to elicit social change. Our hope is through sharing our collective testimonios, we can provide strategies contributing to the practice of liberation for current and future student affairs and higher education professionals of color.

Every paroxysm has the potential to initiate you to something new, giving you a chance to reconstruct yourself, forcing you to rework your description of self, world, and your place in it (reality).

—Gloria E. Anzaldúa (1990, p. 547)

As professionals of color in student affairs, the idea of claiming voice and claiming space frequently comes to question. Understanding the complexity of what it means to thrive within the field of higher education allows us to engage in critical reflection of how we, as student affairs professionals of color, manifest our multifaceted experiences with race, class, gender, and other salient identities. The way in which we make sense of our positionality informs how we decide to show up and how we choose to navigate space. We define space as the context in which we live in, personally and professionally, including the sociopolitical reality of being physically present in space as a person of color.

The unconscious questioning and constant assumption that we must be granted permission to exist in specific spaces within the structure of higher education propels us to form a consciousness termed "liberatory praxis." Liberatory praxis is the practice of engaging in deconstructing notions of oppression while simultaneously permitting ourselves to live out our realities of how we are positioned in society due to the politics of our social identities (Freire, 1972; hooks, 1991). Carrying out a liberatory praxis requires the interweaving of resistance and liberation while, at the same time, acknowledging the way our mind, bodies, and heart carry out knowledge, labor, and the sense of feeling.

As we navigate our position within spaces, we explore the concept of "thriving." We acknowledge that we are positioned within the field of higher education and student affairs, which was not made for the success of black and brown bodies. Furthermore, Black and Brown folks are seen as objects, in addition to, not part of the actual space. We define thriving as the sense of living out an unapologetic reality, which pushes us from thinking about the possibilities to acting on those possibilities. Thriving is a part of engaging in a liberatory praxis.

In this chapter, we interrogate the questioning of spaces we are permitted to claim. We ask ourselves, "What does it mean to thrive in student affairs and higher education?" and "How do we individually and collectively engage in a liberatory praxis?" Our hope is through sharing of our collective testimonios we can provide strategies contributing to the practice of liberation for current and future student affairs and higher education professionals of color.

THEORETICAL EPISTEMOLOGY

The social justice framework of *testimonio* (narrative) guides our efforts in telling our stories. *Testimonio* is the "pedagogical and methodological approach to social justice challenging objectivity by situating the individual in communion with a collective experience marked by marginalization, oppression, or resistance" (Delgado Bernal, Burciaga, & Carmona, 2012, p. 363). Through the use of *testimonios* (narratives) and sharing our truths, we provide stories of how we have come to engage in our individual liberatory praxis. Anzaldúa (1990) captures the idea of claiming voice in theorizing spaces not made for people of color as she speaks on inserting our bodies to disrupt traditional ways of knowing and being because we are often disqualified and excluded from the discourse; thus, it is vital that we do not allow White men and women solely to occupy our theorizing spaces.

SITUATING OUR TESTIMONIOS

As we share our testimonios, it is important to acknowledge the multiple dimensions of our positionalities, defined as the idea that race, class, gender, sexuality, and other forms of social identity "are markers of relational positions" (para. 13) and highlights the way we are positioned in spaces with respect to power, privilege, and oppression (Elliott, 2015). In this particular context, we are positioned both as doctoral students in a higher education program while simultaneously navigating the complexity of our professional student affairs roles on campus. Our realities, as scholar-practitioners, inform our commitment to the transformation of higher education to be more inclusive of people of color. In positioning ourselves to this topic, it is important to understand how each of us shows up when we speak on "thriving."

WHO ARE WE?

Roberto is a native Iowan whose experiences in different regions of the country have informed the way he navigates space. His social position and relationship to space are influenced by his identity as a queer Latinx individual whose contributions to the field of student affairs is guided by his commitment to dismantling oppression in higher education.

DanaMichelle navigates spaces from a lens of being a Black woman from north Jersey. The saliency of her identities informs the way she asserts herself in her position at a highly racially diverse institution.

Tennille, a native of the Bronx, cultivated her passion for social justice in higher education. Her social position as a Black, cisgender woman informs the way she navigates her reality working in predominantly White private institutions.

Cynthia is a native of Lima, Perú whose experiences as a Latina and an immigrant influence how she views diversity and accessibility in higher education. Her commitment to serving underrepresented and silenced minorities are at the core of her professional philosophy.

Lastly, Merylou, as a first-generation college student and Latina, recognizes the power her presence holds in the spaces she occupies for the students she serves. Breaking presumptions of who is considered a scholar and an influential leader in student affairs drive her to continue her work in this field.

In sharing our testimonios with each other, we find shared experiences along with different ways we navigate our lived realities. Thriving as a form of survival and thriving as a form of agency are underlying themes for us. In the next section, we share parts of our stories to give voice to the themes.

THRIVING AS A FORM OF SURVIVAL

As people of color in higher education institutions, we often encounter limitations that influence the way we navigate the profession of student affairs. We, the authors, have dealt with the confines of these challenges within different roles and at various institutions. Despite these boundaries, we enacted ways of thriving not only as a contributor to our success but as a method of survival in the field. Thriving is not a choice, but rather a responsibility to ourselves as a student affairs professional of color that emerges in a multitude of circumstances. An illustration of this ongoing responsibility can be exemplified when considering who has a seat at "the table." The table noted here is defined as the space in which major decisions are being made that significantly impact the institution and its stakeholders. We share the sentiment of our identity as people of color serving as a form of responsibility to bring the voices of communities of color into the space.

> We often come into our respective positions fully aware that our presence and voices are needed in order to represent and advocate for our communities and/or other marginalized ones, which adds personal commitment to our professional experiences. (Cynthia N. Sánchez Gómez)

As highlighted here, our roles include not just our day to day, but an added layer of responsibility to the students who rely on our presence to persist. Thriving in this profession is not only for the sake of ourselves but also for the well-being of our students and colleagues of color.

> Students of color began to gravitate towards me. They camped out in my office and talked to me about anything and everything. I was one of them. I was relatable; I came from the same place they did. It's funny because throughout my career I have heard the same statement "she is one of us" from students in separating me from the "administration," but there is no separation. (Tennille Haynes)

Clearly, based on our experiences, students found solace in us as professionals of color to the extent that we serve as their home base. They come to us for social, professional, and academic support with an understanding that we can relate to their plights. Ultimately, our visible identities and the responsibility for supporting underrepresented groups are what make us claim our voices at "the table."

Beyond the importance of the presence of our voices, the responsibility for serving as role models to underrepresented students emerges as a prevalent theme within our testimonios.

> Not only have I become more aware of the lack of representation in the academe of people of color, but I hadn't realized how, at one point in my life, I'd never considered myself worthy of such aspirations. They always felt out of reach and impossible for someone like me. Working with women from all walks of life in my line of work creates an additional level of accountability that pushes me to strive for success in my work as a future scholar...I can tell my students that their circumstances do not define them but it can build them into the person they hope to become. (Merylou Rodriguez)

Through self-disclosing our identities and experiences, our interaction with students and colleagues tend to become authentic and meaningful given the deep connections we may share. Because of these deep connections, students of color see us as a reflection of themselves, which in turn motivates our drive as professionals. We have a responsibility to thrive in a space where we are often considered guests, yet we do it to transform spaces to validate our collective being.

Therefore, our ability to thrive is not just inherently motivated as we have a responsibility to ourselves, our communities, and the people of color who show up in need of us. By acknowledging our privileged position at "the table," we also recognize the power of bringing knowledge and perspectives that would otherwise not be considered. This recognition is an accessible and effective way in which we can bring the voice of students and colleagues as well as impact the experience of a diverse community. As educators, we are indebted civically to shape our next generation of society that will ultimately make decisions for the future of our world.

Thriving as student affairs professionals of color often becomes synonymous with perfection. Our respective identities do not allow room for error.

> As a mechanism to show my appreciation of their support, I worked overtime and assumed increased job responsibilities well outside of my job description as an academic adviser to accommodate the increasing body of students, but few new hires. (DanaMichelle Harris)

Often we find ourselves overcompensating in our work setting, a practice not commonly shared by our White counterparts. The reasoning behind this type of behavior comes from a concern of not perpetuating negative stereotypes frequently associated with our identities. Despite the unfairness that can result from these types of behaviors, we continue to act this way as though it is the only way to thrive. As seen in our testimonios, we do not feel, want, nor have room to have our work ethic questioned.

In our profession, we see the continued deference given to White colleagues based on a level of presumed intelligence. The validation of who is considered an intellectual and who is not trickles down from the narrow understanding by senior leadership. For many of us, we understand that being considered an intellectual is imperative. Occupying this space requires us to redefine who authenticates knowledge and who gets to create it. Our very presence shatters presumptions of intellect as a White characteristic. Whereas White colleagues are seen merely to be scholarly, we always find ourselves having to prove our credibility.

Therefore, our role in the higher education context becomes that much more critical because we have no choice but to influence change. We allow experiences such as tokenization, when the "means justifies the end," as a benefit for our communities. All things considered, when tangible shifts take place despite these confining circumstances, we take our lack of choice with a sense of ownership.

THRIVING AS A FORM OF AGENCY

In addition to thriving as a form of survival, our testimonies reveal that our consciousness contributes to how we position our individual power to act on behalf of the communities of color in our positions. The onus of establishing comprehensive spaces for students of color becomes the primary responsibility to professionals of color in student affairs that identify with students *on the margins* at predominantly White institutions (PWIs). How we show up in these spaces becomes intentional as our authenticity becomes the mechanism to cultivate the holistic development of both students and colleagues of color who are forced to cope with racialized incidents.

The relationship between the structure of higher education and how we, professionals of color in student affairs, situate ourselves to resist, demand, and transform its culture is taxing. Relationships are supposed to have the capability to influence others; a change in one results in a change in the other. As such, while professionals of student affairs design and develop initiatives to support inclusive environments for students of color, the structure of higher education and student affairs remains a space for White people and we persist in being a bridge between the contrasting spaces. In each opportunity and challenge, we are left to evaluate our sense-of-belongingness to the campus community and our ability to bring about the change we wish to see. It becomes necessary to reposition how we think about the work we do, with whom we do the work, and how to remain committed to speak out against injustice.

We have far more power than we assert in white spaces. Our experiences give voice to the ways the institution is reproducing the transmission of inequality, but we must continue to prioritize respect to facilitate real change.

> I think of being unapologetically conscious and knowing what I bring to the space, whether or not I am seen as valid. Thriving also encompasses knowing when I am not wanted in a way that makes me understand that there are moments when I have to walk away, because my knowledge and sense of being is not deserved in that space. I have to be reminded that sometimes I bring the table to the table, therefore, my responsibility lies in who I give a seat to. (Roberto C. Orozco)

In our profession, there have been times when having a seat at the table has not been enough to continue the work of transforming the landscape of the institution; thus, alternative methods were explored to prove resistance to the normal practices of exclusion that were no longer being accepted.

Thriving as a form of agency in the structure of higher education is emotionally charged. Agency is defined as the expression of individualized power through thoughts, behavior, and voice (Davies, 1991).

> Since entering my doctoral program, I have altered my perspective on my future career goals. Not only have I become more aware of the lack of representation in the academe of people of color, but I hadn't realized how at one point in my life I never considered myself worthy of such aspirations. (Merylou Rodriguez)

Day-to-day interactions with students of color that speak to our own personal journeys provide each of us with the intrinsic reward of being able to be someone to whom students can connect. Yet, being one of the few people of color in our departments, along with the interaction with students of color, becomes a source of contention in our offices with the personal work of which our White co-workers are absolved.

> ...as much as we feel empowered by the idea of becoming role models to students from underrepresented groups, many of us also encounter the realities of alienation and tokenization as we interact with supervisors and/or colleagues. (Cynthia N. Sánchez Gómez)

Despite these professional challenges, we find ways to balance being a vital resource to students of color and maintaining relationships with colleagues so that we can continue to use our seat at the table to advocate on behalf of the students' of color concerns shared with us.

> I remember once sitting in a diversity committee meeting and listening to the members discuss ways in which to acquiring student feedback in focus groups and how to conduct the sessions. When I suggested it might be better not to have staff present so that students would feel more comfortable more honest in their feedback, the assistant dean asked me if I was okay and stated I sounded a bit disgruntled. (Tennille Haynes)

Our experience tells us that we are hired to *deal* with the problem of students of color, not to engage in promoting social change to make the structure of higher education more diverse and inclusive. To thrive in higher education is to move beyond the disappointment of showing up in the space authentically to engage in a one-sided relationship with the institution, but to use our individual power to transform the next generation of student affairs of color to seek out leadership.

STRATEGIES

The purpose of this chapter is to shift from the labor-focused narrative about "what are we doing to dismantle the systems of oppression we function in?" to "how are we thriving in the context in which we are situated and what does claiming voice and space in the multiple context mean?" In providing aspects of our testimonios, we provide strategies, which are not exhaustive, for others to use in their everyday existence within the field of higher education and student affairs.

Build Community Towards Self-Care

Many professionals of color are not afforded the opportunity to show up in a heart space to show what it means to feel the emotions of everyday experiences. The monitoring of our language, movements, and demeanor shifts us into a place of managing our emotions, especially during racialized incidents. It can be isolating and lonely being a person of color in predominantly White spaces. Coping is not a straightforward strategy as it takes strength and resilience. Everyone has their way of coping or developing self-care, but although it takes time to process experiences and emotions, it is important to construct ways of enacting self-care.

One strategy is to seek support on and off campus. For professionals of color, especially for those who exist in all-white spaces (i.e., departments, functional areas), securing support can be difficult. Seeking out faculty and staff groups that center the experiences of people of color is essential for building relationships outside of your functional area. These resource groups help support staff in providing programs, events, and professional development and are great avenues for supporting staff members and assisting with feelings of isolation and alienation. In addition, finding support outside of your campus can be through community and advocacy groups. As one moves into higher leadership positions, these spaces become more prevalent for the continued success of student affairs professionals of color.

Leverage Your Institutional Power

Build and maintain your circle and know your worth as well as what you bring to the table. Reflecting on your salient identities requires internal and interpersonal work that can be painful, but transformational. Specifically for student affairs professionals who are moving within the ranks into higher level leadership, reflecting on identities and building allies can become more difficult due to the limited folks who may identify with your being. We suggest finding ways to acquire opportunities to attend regional or national events where you are able to build relationships across institutions with other folks of color who are also navigating the ranks.

Practice Accountability—When Enough Is Enough

In a speech that General Colin Powell (Northeastern University, 2012) delivered for a university's commencement ceremony, he was asked about his time under the Bush administration. The question was related to how he handled following orders even when he did not agree with the mission. Powell answered that you have to know when to follow and when to leave. Due to the assumed leverage mid-level professionals may have in leaving institutions, knowing when to leave is important. As professionals of color, we are often in conflict with the mission or work of our institutions; but when is enough, enough? When do we decide that morally the situation goes against who we are or conflicts with our values? No one can answer this for you because only you have the power to decide.

Secure Mentorship and Sponsorship

Mentoring is critical to the development and success as well as the continued pipeline of student affairs professionals of color. Mentors are individuals who will help you navigate the field of student affairs, know your everyday experiences, and help shape the vision for your journey, supporting you along every step of the way. Additionally, sponsors are individuals, usually in senior-level leadership, who invest in your success and use their influence to promote and make your work visible. Sometimes, your mentors can also be your sponsors and vice versa. What is important is to acknowledge the support you may be required to voice that need while at the same time building intentional and authentic relationships with individuals who can both mentor and sponsor you.

Sharing our testimonios was intentional in highlighting mechanisms of thriving that have and continue to influence ways in which we claim voice and space. The transformation of student affairs and higher education should not come at the expense of professionals of color, specifically with the burden of taxation often placed on many of us as persons of color. Therefore, as professionals of color in student affairs, it is imperative that we find ways to contribute to thriving towards a liberatory praxis. Carrying out a liberatory praxis requires the interweaving of resistance and liberation, while at the same time acknowledging the way our mind, bodies, and heart carry out knowledge, labor, and feeling.

REFERENCES

Anzaldúa, G. E. (1990). *Making face, making soul/haciendo caras: Creative and critical perspectives of feminists of color.* San Francisco, CA: Aunt Lute Books.

Davies, B. (1991). The concept of agency: A feminist poststructuralist analysis. *Social Analysis: The International Journal of Social and Cultural Practice, 30,* 42–53.

Delgado Bernal, D., Burciaga, R., & Carmona, J. F. (2012). Chicana/Latina testimonios: Mapping the methodological, pedagogical, and political. *Equity & Excellence in Education, 45*(3), 363–372.

Elliott, Z. (2015). *Intersectionality and positionality.* Retrieved from http://www.zettaelliott.com/intersectionalty-positionality/

Freire, P. (1972). *Pedagogy of the oppressed.* New York, NY: Herder and Herder.

hooks, B. (1991). Theory as liberatory practice. *Yale Journal of Law and Feminism, 4*(1), 1–12.

Northeastern University. (2012, May 8). *Colin Powell 2012 commencement speech* [Youtube]. Retrieved from https://www.youtube.com/watch?v=xtf6VQSBJAs

CHAPTER 14

THE WORDS THAT SET US FREE

Storytelling as Praxis for Student Affairs Professionals of Color

Allison C. Roman
Trinity University

Grounded in Black feminist thought, Latina/Chicana feminist frameworks, critical race theory, scholarly personal narratives, and testimonios, storytelling can be utilized as a practice for engaging effectively and authentically for professionals of color, creating a space for liberation, healing, and joy. The author discusses how storytelling practices can collectively shape and transform individuals and policies to be reflective and responsive to the lived experiences of professionals of color.

Storytelling has been used as tool and process within communities of color, especially as a way to affirm and validate one's lived experiences (Banks-Wallace, 1998). Storytelling allows for communities of color to share their experiences in "their own voice" to define their reality, giving meaning to their journey (Reyes, 2011) and creates a sphere of theorized existence (Amoah,

No Ways Tired, pages 131–139
Copyright © 2019 by Information Age Publishing
All rights of reproduction in any form reserved.

1998). I argue that, similarly, storytelling can be used as a mechanism for understanding the lived experiences of student affairs professionals of color in addition to serving as a vehicle for social and institutional change.

STORYTELLING AS CREATION OF KNOWLEDGE

To understand storytelling as praxis for student affairs professionals of color, we must understand the context storytelling has been used, specifically in understanding the experiences of students of color. Grounded in critical race theory (CRT), storytelling is a means to draw on the experiences of communities of color and hold them as creators of knowledge. While communities of color "are holders and creators of knowledge, they often feel as if their histories, experiences, cultures, and languages are devalued, misinterpreted, or omitted within formal educational settings" (Delgado Bernal, 2002, p. 390).

Storytelling in CRT is a response to the deficit models in which stories about marginalized communities are told, and views stories as a strength with the ability to empower marginalized communities as experts of their lived experiences. In addition to CRT and education research, storytelling as a tool is present in Black feminist thought and Chicana and Latina feminism. Through the application of an intersectional lens, one can explore and unpack the experiences of women of color through a lens that highlights the ways that race, gender, and other marginalized identities shape one's experience. In Black feminist frameworks, storytelling and narratives are a critical methodology. As a tradition and practice, storytelling allows for women of color to create space for them and their specific experiences. Through a Black feminism and Chicana/Latina approach, narratives create a theoretical frame where the physical realities of our lives can serve as a bridge that contradicts their experiences (Moraga & Anzaldua, 2015).

In Chicana and Latina feminist works, storytelling or *testimonios* reveal the ways in which the experiences of racism, patriarchy, xenophobia, documented status, and more are realized. Generational differences are also able to be explored. The process of *testimonio* builds from the lived experiences of people of color to...theorize [their] oppression (Perez-Huber, 2009) and through this process, we become experts of our own lives.

STORYTELLING FOR HEALING

Storytelling can be a site of healing, affirmation, and validation. Sharing personal narratives can decrease the sense of isolation in professional and social environments (Banks-Wallace, 2002). It is in these spaces where these stories can be used to bond, build community, and heal. As Banks-Wallace described, storytelling has been used by women to vent emotions they had little opportunity to express in their daily lives (Banks-Wallace, 2002). Storytelling allows us to understand the roots of our oppression and as a result, provides language for our experiences. To be seen and feel affirmed in one's existence heals and liberates people because it allows them to survive in a system that deems them as less than. Storytelling within a community also provides us the collective strength to work toward our liberation.

STORYTELLING AS SITES OF RESISTANCE AND LIBERATION

What makes storytelling especially powerful is how it counters the narratives created by dominant structures. The process of storytelling shifts from what is prioritized as objective to elevating the validity of the subjective. Objectivity operates as a characteristic of white supremacy culture (Jones & Okun, 2001) and seeks to delegitimize experiences that are not considered objective or facts. What is considered objective is established by dominant culture (i.e., White supremacy, patriarchy, heteronormativity, etc.) and renders the experiences of marginalized and disenfranchised communities invisible or irrelevant. For marginalized communities, storytelling becomes intellectual tools used to fight back against assumed and constructed invisibility, powerlessness, and voicelessness (Hua, 2013).

I will employ scholarly personal narratives (SPN), which allows for the first person narrative truth and reimagining from a personal perspective to highlight pivotal moments that impacted me as a student affairs professional of color and how storytelling became a catalyst to make meaning of my experience, my identity, and my career. I will then extrapolate the potential of storytelling in shifting organizational cultures to positively impact the experiences of student affairs professionals of color.

EXPERIENCES OF PROFESSIONALS OF COLOR

If you were to ask me how I ended up in student affairs, my story would probably mirror those of some of my colleagues—I kind of just fell into it. The first time I even considered a career in student affairs was the last semester of my master's program. I was studying social work with an emphasis in community organization with children and youth. I knew I wanted to work in the educational system, but it didn't occur to me that a career in student affairs was even an option. What I knew was that I wanted to make college more accessible and equitable for students of color, first-generation college students, and students from low-socioeconomic statuses.

My first job out of graduate school was an assistant director for our campus' multicultural affairs office. This role allowed me to not only work with pre-college programs but to also work with students of color on campus. I was entrenched in the issues my students were experiencing while simultaneously experiencing some issues of my own.

As a first-generation college student, my experiences were greatly shaped by my view of race, gender, and socioeconomic status. I struggled academically and socially to find my place at a prestigious, tier one, research institution. I suffered in silence and felt isolated in my undergraduate experience. My feelings of inadequacy, isolation, and embarrassment followed me through my graduate experience and the beginning of my career as a student affairs professional. In addition to my assigned job duties, I carried my identities as I navigated through this predominantly White institution (PWI). I began feeling inundated with social justice issues both at work and in my personal life. How naïve of me to think that I, as a woman of color, could separate the two.

My experiences as a professional mirrored the experiences my students faced. I experienced feeling tokenized as a Latina, rendered invisible as a Black woman, and dealt with microaggressions from colleagues and other students. I often longed for spaces where I could share these experiences with other professionals. I eventually found those spaces. Two incidents in particular illustrate how my students and I experienced racial traumas and found space to share our feelings and reassure each other.

November 25, 2014: The Non-Indictment of Darren Wilson

We were glued to our television, watching as the St. Louis county prosecutor announced that the grand jury decided not to indict Ferguson police officer Darren Wilson for murdering teenager, Michael Brown. I had been following this event closely, especially in light of other cases of police brutality post-Trayvon Martin. However, this time, the agony I felt was like the straw that had broken the camel's back. I mourned for the Black and Latino children I had not yet had, and I sobbed because this was not new or surprising. I have been here before and I knew I would be here again.

June 18, 2015: Charleston Massacre

It was late at night and I was doing what I normally did before I went to bed—I checked Facebook. I saw an article posted on my feed, "Shooting in Charleston, Nine Dead." After realizing it was not a hoax and as more details began to pour out, my heart ached. I was horrified and I sobbed as I thought of all the times I had been at my own predominantly Black church. I tried to go to sleep knowing that my students would need me the next day. In moments like these, my office became a refuge, a space for my students to cry and yell "Why do they keep killing us?" I provided space for them but I was growing weary and tired.

The day after each of these horrific events, I went to work expecting to find others who were shaken to their core, faces that resembled mine—hopeless, defeated, and just damn tired. But as I walked across campus at this PWI, everyone seemed happy. It seemed as if it were any other day. The conversations I overheard bared no mention of what had been happening in the news. There was no mention of the atrocities I witnessed. It felt as if I had been living in an alternative universe where only I could see what was happening. For a moment, I felt so alone. However, later on in the day, I would find familiar faces that looked like mine and as we would see each other, we would embrace. Sometimes, words weren't spoken and we would sometimes cry. During these times, other student affairs colleagues of color and I would somehow find our way to each other. These spaces became the locations on campus where we could share stories of collective grief, mourning, fear, but also stories of community and resilience. Stories took us out from isolation and became sites where we could grapple with the reality of simultaneously having to support our students while grieving ourselves.

These weren't the only instances in which our personal and professional experiences came crashing together. In supporting my students, I realized that I was beginning to feel burnt out. I was vicariously experiencing their racial traumas all while trying to cope with my own, which led to feelings of racial battle fatigue that includes increased levels of psychosocial stressors and subsequent psychological, physiological, and behavioral responses due to fighting racial microaggressions (Smith, Hung, & Franklin, 2011). Thankfully, storytelling has been a means to begin to alleviate the additional burden student affairs professionals of color are expected to carry.

STORYTELLING AS PRAXIS

Storytelling can be used in support of professionals of color, undergraduate and graduate students, and the individual. The practice of storytelling can collectively shape and transform strategies and policies to be reflective and responsive to the lived experiences of professionals of color.

Storytelling for Professionals

As a student affairs professional of color, storytelling became a space for me and others to feel affirmed in our experiences. Through town halls or professional networking groups, creating a space to share stories has been vital to our collective well-being. I have found that in conference spaces or online digital spaces, telling our stories has led to the creation of networks that provide us refuge. In these spaces, using humor in how we tell our stories has been important as well. Telling our story as professionals provides us the catharsis needed to sustain ourselves within our institutions (Banks-Wallace, 1998).

Storytelling With Students

In using storytelling in my work with students of color, I developed an activity where my students had to imagine their life as a book and tasked with creating a title as well as titles for chapters that highlighted pivotal moments in their lives. In these moments, I also shared with them that I was the first one in my family to attend college, with my entire family looking at me as the example for my younger siblings and cousins. So when I failed my first semester with a 0.33 GPA, I was ashamed. Up until that moment, only my parents and the dean that gave me a second chance had known. However, after I finished sharing, my students began to share their own stories with some acknowledging how they felt moved to share their experiences because of what I had modeled. I began to understand how grappling with my own story served as a model for my students to share their own. Another memorable moment is when a Latina student informed me that she heard the story about my failing my first semester of college, revealing that she too had failed her first semester and experienced feelings of defeat. Through my story, we were able to bond and discuss strategies so that she could succeed and not feel weighed down by her past performance.

Storytelling can also shape the experiences of students of color in graduate programs preparing for a career in student affairs, particularly as they tend to lack representation in the classroom. Generally, students of color in higher education and student affairs programs experience racial microaggressions perpetuated by peers, faculty, and assistantship supervisors who are well-meaning (Linder, Harris, Allen, & Hubain, 2015). By exploring the experiences and stories of future student affairs professionals of color, we can begin to understand the ways in which oppression continues and thrives in higher education.

Storytelling for Support and Mentoring

In addition to bonding, storytelling allows communities to create sites of resistance for marginalized communities to counter the narratives told about them. I facilitated a program for women of color on our campus, the NIARA mentoring program, that provided a space to both students as well as professional women of color to discuss their racialized and gendered experiences within the context of a PWI. During one of our regular monthly meetings, we were discussing how under the guise of professionalism, people of color may be deemed as unprofessional in regards to their natural hair in addition to conversations about code-switching; feeling exhaustion due to navigating multiple spaces as women of color; and balancing the fine line of advocating for themselves while not seeming too aggressive or angry. There was catharsis and affirmation as several different identities of women of color, from different backgrounds, ages, education levels, and positions on campus, shared similar stories that tied our intergenerational experiences together.

In another NIARA meeting, I facilitated a conversation with students regarding the narratives written about women of color and the stereotypes their identities carried. Some of them flat out refused the narratives imposed on them and some embraced them as a way to reclaim something that had been deemed as negative by societal standards. For example, one student shared how being "ratchet" was something she was proud of, how she sought to shatter the notions of respectability, and how she was expected to move and live in this world. In the meeting, I asked them to write a letter to themselves and to another women of color, sharing them with one another upon completion. During this process, there were heads nodding, an echo of snaps comforting each student as they read their truth, and tears of relief from releasing the burdens they once carried.

Inspired by the aforementioned meetings, I launched "Dear Sis," an online space for women of color to share their stories in various creative forms. I also created a space for women of color directors who work in the areas of diversity, inclusion, and social justice to share their stories. To be in the virtual presence of other women of color in order to share our narratives allows us to share tools for navigating and resisting oppressive structures that impact us as women of color.

If storytelling is to be used as a liberatory practice that acknowledges the inequities perpetuated in higher education institutions as praxis for support, it is important to first acknowledge that the historical roots of higher education was not built for people of color. It is important to note that storytelling should not be used to tokenize the experiences or hold one person of color as the sole voice on issues related to marginalized communities. Stories should be collected and heard from multiple voices from a variety of experiences. It's a delicate balance but the intent should not perpetuate what tends to happen—having a singular voice that represents all marginalized communities.

Storytelling for Self and Others

In addition, to fully understand our stories, we must take an intersectional approach. For example, my experience as a Black Latina woman is deeply shaped by White supremacy, capitalism, misogynoir, colorism, and patriarchy. As I began meeting other Black Latinas, specifically student affairs professionals, we explored our stories and historias together. Through the process of sharing our stories, we began to understand how our experiences have been shaped by various systems of oppression. For example, we have discussed how as light skinned Black Latinas, we have been afforded the opportunity to speak about our issues in a way that may not be afforded to dark-skinned Black Latinas. Through sharing our stories, we weave together the commonalities of our experiences and make sense of our experiences. We also have been able to increase the visibility of those with similar identities, specifically in the context of higher education.

CONCLUSION

Storytelling can transform how communities of color are discussed in the context of higher education, especially since higher education professionals can sometimes operate in silos as it relates to identity. There may be spaces based on an individual's identity, but for those with multiple marginalized identities, one may be forced to make a choice. We must use stories to identify the barriers that impede the success of professionals of color. We must also recognize how racial battle fatigue impacts various communities of color. When listening to stories, we must acknowledge others' stories as their truth. For storytelling to be impactful, it is important to remove the barriers that would prevent a culture of storytelling from being fully realized (e.g., the fear of retaliation for exposing inequities within higher education or being tokenized).

By bringing student affairs professionals of color together to share their stories, therein lies an opportunity to facilitate support and healing, especially around our marginalized identities. Spaces for professionals of color as well as networks and caucuses for Black and Latino professionals in student affairs, including digital spaces like the Black Student Affairs Professionals (BLKSAP) Facebook group, can serve as sites of healing and building community.

In conclusion, it is important to note that storytelling alone cannot solve the inequities in higher education. However, it can be used to shed light on the experiences of student affairs professionals of color. By centering and legitimizing the stories and narratives of professionals of color, then maybe our words can be heard then maybe our words can set us free.

REFERENCES

Amoah, J. (1997). Narrative: The road to black feminist theory. *Berkeley Women's Law Journal, 12,* 84–102.

Banks-Wallace, J. (1998). Emancipatory potential of storytelling in a group. *Journal of Nursing Scholarship, 30,* 17–21.

Delgado Bernal, D. (2002). Critical race theory, Latino critical theory, and critical raced-gendered epistemologies: Recognizing students of color as holders and creators of knowledge. *Qualitative Inquiry, 8,* 105–126.

Hua, A. (2013). Black diaspora feminism and writing: Memories, storytelling, and the narrative world as sites of resistance. *African and Black Diaspora: An International Journal, 6,* 30–42.

Jones, K., & Okun, T. (2001). *White supremacy culture—Dismantling racism: A workbook for social change groups.* Retrieved from http://www.goldenbridgesschool.org/uploads/1/9/5/4/19541249/white_supremacy_culture__1_.pdf

Linder, C., Harris, J. C., Allen, E. L., & Hubain, B. (2015). Building inclusive pedagogy: Recommendations from a national study of students of color in higher education and student affairs graduate programs. *Equity & Excellence in Education, 48,* 178–194.

Moraga, C., & Anzaldúa, G. (1981). *This bridge called my back: Writings by radical women of color* (4th ed.). Albany, NY: State of New York Press.

Perez Huber, L. (2009). Disrupting apartheid of knowledge: Testimonio as methodology in Latina/o critical race research in education. *International Journal of Qualitative Studies in Education, 22,* 639–654.

Reyes L.-V. (2011). A testimonio of a Latino male professional journey. In L. W. Watson & C. S. Woods (Eds.), *Go where you belong: Male teachers as cultural workers in the lives of children, families, and communities* (pp. 83–89). Rotterdam, The Netherlands: Sense.

Smith, W., Hung, M., Franklin, J. D., (2011). Racial battle fatigue and the misEducation of Black men: Racial microaggressions, societal problems, and environmental stress. *The Journal of Negro Education, 80*(1), 63–82.

CHAPTER 15

A HOMECOMING OF SORTS

Richard Song
University of Rhode Island

Shirley M. Consuegra
University of Rhode Island

John C. Cruz
University of Rhode Island

In order for higher education institutions to recruit and retain staff of color, administrators need to pay attention to their experiences. In this chapter, the authors, who identify as mid-level professionals, provide narratives beginning with their journey as undergraduate students at a predominantly White institution (PWI). Now serving as full-time staff members at their alma mater, the authors reflect on the progress that has been made as it relates to diversity, inclusion, and equity, while acknowledging the work that still needs to be done. Through a dialogic format, the authors hope to offer readers some insight into how conversation, community, and the creation of counterspaces can help staff of color not only survive at a PWI, but also thrive.

No Ways Tired, pages 141–150
Copyright © 2019 by Information Age Publishing
All rights of reproduction in any form reserved.

Institutions of higher education maintain that diversity and inclusion are core values for their campus community. Moreover, research (Smith, 2015; Williams, Berger, & McClendon, 2005) suggests that a diverse educational setting is critical to the intellectual and personal growth of its members. The U.S. Department of Education (2015) states that:

> Professionals of color help create diverse learning environments to help students sharpen their critical thinking and analytical skills; prepare students to succeed in an increasingly diverse and interconnected world; break down stereotypes and reduce bias; and enable schools to fulfill their role in opening doors for students of all backgrounds. (p. 25)

Because of the role professionals of color play on college campuses, it has become increasingly important to examine how they not only help students of color navigate their experiences at PWIs, but also how they steer through those same spaces as employees and support each other along the way. Although professionals of color spend time and energy helping underrepresented students navigate complex systems, many, however, come into the profession with little to no guidance on how to navigate oppressive systems and manage their own reactions to White spaces. To mitigate this discrepancy, it is important that attention is given to the current experiences of professionals of color if an institution is truly committed to creating and sustaining diverse learning environments.

Oppressive systems involve unequal access to resources that have negative impacts on communities of color. Research has shown that conversations between colleagues from marginalized identities (Jones 2009; Nicolazzo & Harris, 2014) and the creation of counterspaces (Mena & Vaccaro, 2017; Ong, Smith, & Ko, 2017) help foster relationships with those who may share similar experiences and can help counter negative impacts. In this chapter, collective stories serve at the heart of illustrating the importance of building community through conversations and finding counterspaces that heal the heart and replenish the soul. Strategies for survival are offered rooted in the authors' experiences at one PWI as students and then professionals, as history is the best teacher.

SHIRLEY: I CAN BE LATINX AND BLACK?

My love affair with my current institution started my senior year in high school. In the fall of 1992, students from marginalized groups staged a peaceful protest and presented administration with *Fourteen Demands* addressing the oppressive conditions on campus. My sister was a first-year student and witnessed this impressive student movement. As a 17-year-old, Black, Latinx coming from a predominantly White high school, I was in awe of this community of students and the power of their collective voice. A year later, I began my undergraduate experience with this event as the backdrop to my story.

Until this point in my life, I had never really questioned my identity, especially my Blackness and what that meant in the world. In the Latinx community, we do not talk about our African roots. During this time, I came of age and began to understand my history and my blackness and what these two spheres meant on a college campus and in the world beyond campus. I began to understand my intersecting identities—Black, Latinx, female, first-generation college student—and injustices in a different light. I was fortunate to have people and spaces that allowed me to explore and process my emotions. I found a safe haven in the relationships I made with other students of color and student organizations. I found refuge in the African American studies courses I took and in the relationship I cultivated with the department chair. I found shelter in the college access program I was a part of that supported students from disadvantaged backgrounds. I found a sense of peace in the mentoring relationship I established with my advisor from that program. I found a community that affirmed who I was and counterspaces that gave me support I needed to survive and thrive.

Upon graduation, I stayed on campus as an Americorps VISTA member. In an instant, I went from being a student of color to a staff of color at the PWI. As a student, I learned to advocate for myself, to call out injustices when I experienced them, and to help move forward a social justice agenda. Now as a staff member, I was different. I did not know how to be that person in my new role. Microaggressions were as commonplace in the office as they were in the classroom, but I had not learned how to navigate these experiences with co-workers. For many, my Latinx identity was acceptable but not my Blackness, often hearing, "But Shirley you are not Black." Building community takes time and without those relationships in place, I felt lost. Three years later, I left the university.

As life would have it, I returned to the university 14 years later. The university looked different and now offered some of the things students, staff, and faculty of color had fought for over the years since my departure. The university now had Africana studies as a major; an office of community, equity and diversity; and an increased student of color population. I was ready to engage and become part of a community that had embraced the struggles of the community of color and was working towards a more just and equitable campus. But despite these changes, the campus felt a lot like it did when I was an undergraduate. The best way for me to summarize this feeling is to say that a colleague recently said, "But I just don't see you as Black Shirley."

JOHN: HOW CAN I USE MY VOICE?

My journey at the institution began at birth as I was the child of two first-year students. My mother was an in-state student admitted through an access program for students from disadvantaged backgrounds. My father was an out-of-state student, and eventual captain of the basketball team, whose aspirations of having a professional career in the sport were derailed after a devastating injury. Growing up, I spent a great deal of time on campus as my mother went on to hold a summer campus position. Throughout the years, I developed an affinity for the institution and knew that I too wished to attend.

I entered the institution in 1998 through the same access program as my mother. A few weeks into my first semester, I realized there was a need for additional support for students of color when I was invited to attend a weekly meeting for males of color. These weekly meetings served as a support group where students met to discuss issues and concerns. As one of two first-year students in the group, I did much more observing than contributing as the plights of my fellow group members began to shape my view of the institution.

After a few months, we moved from a support group to a group of action when multiple acts of racial discrimination occurred on campus. We aimed to make campus not only more equitable, but also a place where students of color could flourish. Our advocacy helped create scholarships for students in need, new faculty and staff positions, curricular change that better reflected our population, and an increased number of students admitted into the access program. The movement was broad in terms of diversity, reaching beyond the African-American experience to support other marginalized groups.

When I returned to the institution as a graduate student in 2009, my goal was to serve as an advisor for the access program that was responsible for both my and my mother's higher education experience. This goal changed as a result of my studies. While I remained passionate about serving this population, I realized I could affect more change by working in other areas where students normally did not see staff of color. I would then be a welcoming face to support all students from disadvantaged backgrounds rather than just a selected group.

Years later, I found myself fighting similar battles on the same campus but now as a staff member. As an introvert heavily entrenched in the political leadership framework (Bolman & Deal, 2015) who does work that is highly collaborative in nature, I have found ways to use my voice and speak truth to power. I have been a part of formal initiatives (e.g., committees and commissions), but felt limited by institutional structure and culture. Conversely, I found that my collegial nature and ability to bring people together have been more beneficial as I have connected like-minded individuals of varying experience. Oftentimes, I find myself individually processing through issues shortly after they have taken place and then rallying individuals in my counterspace (Vaccaro & Camba-Kelsay, 2016) to be deliberate and take action.

RICHARD: AM I THE MODEL MINORITY?

As a first-generation college student, my first exposure to a college campus was at orientation. I am a proud product of the same access program previously mentioned. My experience as a student of color and a member of the LGBTQ community was ordinary. I went to class, made friends, and got involved. Perhaps my collegiate experience was ordinary because I surrounded myself with people who were respectful of my journey. In class or in my social circles, I was never asked to give the "gay" or "Asian" perspective. When I volunteered my response, I prefaced my answer stating, "I do not speak for all members of the LGBTQ nor Asian communities." Moreover, fate gave me a mentor. My mentor, a straight, White female, who was invested in my undergraduate experience. She gave me opportunities to become involved and shaped me to become the professional I am today. I firmly believe she sheltered me from knowing the politics of higher education and its implications for the community of color. I now wonder if the opportunities I had as an undergraduate were a result of my Asian identity, the model minority illusion (Tatum, 1997).

It was not until graduate school that I learned about systems of oppression. The courses opened my eyes to seeing the world through a different lens and taught me to critically look at the world around me. I was naïve as an undergraduate as I took everything for what it was and never questioned policies. I thought, "This is the policy, I should respect it." As a Cambodian-American, I was taught to never question authorities. Asking "why" is viewed as disrespectful. In 2009, I graduated with my master's degree and moved around the country in several professional positions. In 2013, I returned to my alma mater.

It was not until my current position that I saw how inequities manifest in policies and interpersonal interactions. I now see and feel the impact of microaggressions. When I first heard the comment, "You know what they say about Asian drivers," it felt surreal. I have read about such instances, but really could not fathom that such actions happened. I was stunned and walked away. Reflecting on it, should I have confronted the individual? Maybe I should have; but this person held a lot of power. At that moment, I felt that I was not in a place to challenge this individual. Would I approach this situation differently if this happened again? Of course I would, especially now since I have a counterspace that provides me with the tools to challenge such statements.

COMING TOGETHER FOR CONVERSATION, COMMUNITY, AND COUNTERSPACES

As demographics continue to change and more staff of color are working at institutions of higher education (Garcia & Serrata, 2016), college campuses have a responsibility to make their environments welcoming, inclusive, and equitable. Wheatley (2009) offered a starting point for creating change in stating, "Human conversation is the most ancient and easiest way to cultivate the conditions for change-personal change, community and organizational change, planetary change" (p.7). In order to create change, institutions must create structured opportunities for dialogue and foster an environment in which community members have space for conversations about things that matter to them.

In the following section, the authors draw on the power of human conversation. Using a dialogic format, they share their perspectives on having conversations, building community, and finding counterspaces.

Question: *What are the barriers that prevent staff of color from taking part in conversations that impact the student, staff, and faculty experience?*

Richard: A barrier I see as I sit around the table with campus partners who provide students with experiential learning opportunities is the lack of staff of color at the table. Aside from me, everyone is White. How do we help students of color find these opportunities when the people around the table do not look like them nor share their experiences? Staff of color are not being hired for key positions that can help impact the experiences of the community of color.

Shirley: I think a real barrier is fear. I have learned over the years that unless people from the dominant culture have some personal experience or know someone of color to whom they feel connected, they are not going to move an agenda or give up their power for the sake of change. This realization meant that I had to have the courage to share my experiences and often be the person to make others in the room feel uncomfortable. Such action puts you in a vulnerable place and it can be scary at first to challenge colleagues.

John: One of the barriers I struggle with most is the reactionary nature of this work. Oftentimes, we are not having these conversations campus-wide until an incident occurs that impacts the community of color. Conversations about race and inclusion need to be an everyday occurrence and not just as a response to an incident.

The aforementioned barriers make it challenging to have authentic conversations about inclusion. If they choose, institutions of higher education can create opportunities for staff of color to share their stories, which in turn can help inform policies and practices that are more inclusive. Conversations about issues of social justice are hard and can often feel messy for individuals. Wheatley (2009) reminds us that "because conversation is the natural way that humans think together, it is, like all life, messy. Life doesn't move in straight lines and neither does a good conversation" (p. 36). Such conversations can be a part of everyday discourse in higher education by providing a structured, thoughtful "Critical Conversation Series" embedded in existing structures such as human resources training, department retreats, professional development, committees and staff meetings.

Structured opportunities to have conversations and connect individuals on campus can help build a sense of community. In the book, *Can We Talk About Race? And Other Conversations in an Era of School Resegregation*, Dr. Beverly Tatum (2007) described the importance of building community in creating inclusive learning environments for students of color. This concept can also be applied to creating inclusive work environments for staff of color. According to Tatum, building community means, "creating a community in which everyone has a sense of belonging, a community in which there are shared norms and values as well as a sense of common purpose that unites its members" (p. 22).

Question: *What are some of the challenges you face when building community?*

Richard: A challenge to building community is the slowness of the institution's response to an incident that impacts the community of color on campus. This lagging shows that addressing incidents and supporting certain communities are not a priority. Every minute that goes by that we do not hear from administration sends a powerful message of, "You are less than me or I do not have time for you."

Shirley: High staff turnover and fatigue are some of the challenges I see when it comes to building community. Creating community takes time, energy, and persistence. I spent a lot of time in my early years being the eager person who wanted to add programs hoping to change oppressive structures and build community. Over time, I realized I was adding things that could easily be deleted while never really impacting the structures already in place. Structural changes are big battles to fight. These battles often leave staff of color exhausted, and for some, leads them to leave their positions.

John: I have had opportunities to be on the front lines of challenging some of the campus offices that are designed to support us. Those have not been easy experiences for me. Part of the challenge is the work that comes out of these offices is always well-intentioned, but often not action-oriented. Change happens when we act. Too often I have been a part of committees that seemingly meet-to-meet instead of meeting-to-do. This leads to frustration.

Despite the challenges building community presents, there are ways professionals of color can be more intentional about providing platforms that foster community building. Building community takes time. Institutions and individuals must invest resources in order to provide the time and space for its members to come together.

Although building community can lead to a sense of belonging, the process can be long and can feel exhausting and painful to staff of color in PWIs. Oftentimes, counterspaces are created as a response (McConnell, Todd, Odahl-Ruan, & Shattell, 2016) because they offer individuals with marginalized identities a safe space to tell their stories and process negative experiences (Vaccaro & Camba-Kelsay, 2016). Counterspaces are also used for individuals to vent their frustrations, offer support, and engage in reflection. It is recommended that these kinds of spaces be identified, created, and supported as a resource for communities of color who work at PWIs. If these spaces do not exist, creating affinity groups by members of the identified marginalized groups can be a starting point.

Question: *In what ways can staff of color employ counterspaces when navigating oppressive systems?*

Richard: Creating events that serve as counterspaces is a good start. Hosting a conference for professionals of color on campus could offer a place of refuge to build community and share stories. Affinity groups can also be another way to create counterspaces.

Shirley: We need to lean on each other and build support that travels with us through our interactions on campus. When you are the only person of color in the room, having that counterspace allows you to go to a place and say, "This just happened and I didn't know how to respond and I need help processing through it." Sometimes when you leave a space after experiencing microaggressions, you feel out of sorts and having a counterspace can help.

John: My coping mechanism around messy conversations has changed. Years ago, I would have swept stuff under the rug or have been that naïve person and said "Okay, that happened. Business as usual." Now, I find my counterspace(s). I go home and think about what transpired in a meeting and I share my thoughts and feelings with people in my counterspace(s). These conversations sometimes lead to action. Knowing I have safe space(s) to go to and bounce ideas off has been helpful for me because action can come from sharing with others.

CONCLUSION

For the authors, work in higher education is more than a career, it is a way of life. As they recall their experiences in a place that taught them a lot about who they are and what their existence means in the world, they feel fortunate to have the opportunity to return to this place and provide that same space to the next generation of students of color. It was in this very space that they first learned that conversation unites us, community sustains us, and counterspaces give us the energy to keep going, even in the darkest of hours. As Turner (2015) indicated,

> Chances to learn and understand one another do exist, but for real change to take place, individuals must have opportunities to interact with others from different backgrounds and be open to the incorporation of new and unfamiliar ways of thinking. (p. 352)

As college campuses work to embody their values of diversity and inclusion, it will be important to pause and recognize the lived experiences of their community of color and for professionals of color to have their voices heard.

REFERENCES

Bolman, L. G., & Deal, T. E. (2017). *Reframing organizations: Artistry, choice, and leadership.* Hoboken, NJ: Wiley.

Garcia, J., & Serrata, W. (2016). Meeting the challenge of demographic change. *The Chronicle of Higher Education.* Retrieved from https://www.chronicle.com/article/Meeting-the-Challenge-of/238582

Jones, S. R. (2009). Constructing identities at the intersections: An autoethnographic exploration of multiple dimensions of identity. *Journal of College Student Development, 50*(3), 287–304. http://doi.org/10.1353/csd.0.0070

McConnell, E. A., Todd, N. R., Odahl-Ruan, C., & Shattell, M. (2016). Complicating counterspaces: Intersectionality and the Michigan womyn's music festival. *American Journal of Community Psychology, 57*(4), 473–488. http://doi.org/10.1002/ajcp.12051

Mena, J. A., & Vaccaro, A. (2017). "I've struggled, I've battled": Invisibility microaggressions experienced by women of color at a predominantly White institution. *The Journal About Women in Higher Education, 10*(3), 301–318. https://doi.org/10.1080/19407882.2017.1347047

Nicolazzo, Z., & Harris, C. (2014). This is what a feminist (space) looks like: (Re)conceptualizing women's centers as feminist spaces in higher education. *About Campus, 18*(6), 2–9. https://doi.org/10.1002/abc.21138

Ong, M., Smith, J. M., & Ko, L. T. (2018). Counterspaces for women of color in STEM higher education: Marginal and central spaces for persistence and success. *Journal of Research in Science Teaching, 55*, 206–245. https://doi.org/10.1002/tea.21417

Smith, D. G. (2015). *Diversity's promise for higher education: Making it work* (2nd ed.). Baltimore, MD: Johns Hopkins University Press.

Tatum, B. D. (1997). *Why are all the black kids sitting together in the cafeteria? And other conversations about race.* New York, NY: Basic Books.

Tatum, B. D. (2007). *Can we talk about race? And other conversations in an era of school resegregation.* Boston, MA: Bacon Press.

Turner, C. S. (2015). Lessons from the field: Cultivating nurturing environments in higher education. *The Review of Higher Education, 38*(3), 333–358. https://doi.org/10.1353/rhe.2015.0023

U.S. Department of Education. (2015). *Protecting civil rights, advancing equity: Report to the president and secretary of education.* Retrieved from https://www2.ed.gov/about/reports/annual/ocr/report-to-president-and-secretary-of-education-2013-14.pdf

Vaccaro, A., & Camba-Kelsay, M. J. (2016). *Centering women of color in academic counterspaces: A critical race analysis of teaching, learning, and classroom dynamics.* Lanham, MD: Lexington Books.

Wheatley, M. J. (2009). *Turning to one another: Simple conversations to restore hope to the future.* San Francisco, CA: Berrett-Koehler.

Williams, D. A., Berger, J. B., & McClendon, S. A. (2005). *Toward a model of inclusive excellence and change in postsecondary institutions.* Washington, DC: Association of American Colleges and Universities.

CHAPTER 16

TRANSCENDING THE IMPOSTER PHENOMENON AS A MULTIRACIAL PROFESSIONAL

Ashley Spicer-Runnels
Texas A&M University–San Antonio

As the community of student affairs professionals becomes more diverse, professionals must learn to manage the effects of imposter syndrome and other identity characteristics that stifle potential. Imposter phenomenon refers to a person's belief that they are a fraud and associated with a fear of being exposed as inadequate. As a result, the imposter phenomenon has a direct impact on the way they survive and thrive as student affairs professional. This chapter provides strategies, based on my lived experiences, to transcend the impact of the imposter syndrome, multiracial identity, and common student affairs attrition factors. These strategies include navigating systems, integration, and commitment to self, which lead to knowledge acquisition and the ability to take calculated risks.

No Ways Tired, pages 151–156
Copyright © 2019 by Information Age Publishing
All rights of reproduction in any form reserved.

Millennials are often criticized for aspiring to advance too quickly without adequate experience and while this may be accurate in some cases, there are many young professionals who have advanced to administrative positions and achieved successes but feel like imposters. This feeling, known as imposter phenomenon (Clance & Imes, 1978), refers to a person's belief that they are a fraud or phony. These individuals often fear being exposed as inadequate and hold themselves to exceptionally high standards. As a result, the imposter phenomenon has a direct impact on the way they survive and thrive as student affairs professionals.

INTERNAL AND EXTERNAL PROFESSIONAL INFLUENCES

A professional's attempt to survive and thrive within a campus community can quickly be extinguished by internal and external influences. The psychological impact of the imposter syndrome, combined with common attrition factors and characteristics associated with identity, can influence how an individual navigates their career. Clance and Imes' (1978) found that highly successful women, who despite their accomplishments and competence, discounted their intellect and as a result, coined the term imposter phenomenon. While imposter phenomenon was originally and extensively studied in high-achieving women and later expanded to other college student samples including graduate and undergraduate students (Clance & Imes, 1978; Gibson-Beverly & Schwartz, 2008), newer studies have examined the impact on higher education faculty and professionals (Hutchins, 2015). Furthermore, while some research has found that the imposter phenomenon was higher among women than men, other studies have failed to produce gender differences (Cokley, McClain, Enciso, & Martinez, 2013; Cowman & Ferrari, 2002). While a certain amount of self-doubt is normal in any position, Hutchins (2015) explained that individuals experiencing imposter phenomenon tended to have heightened anxiety associated with taking credit for their successes.

Although some professionals endure, the impact of the imposter phenomenon often results in professionals exiting the industry. The subject of attrition within the profession of student affairs has continued to interest professionals and researchers for decades (Renn & Jessup-Anger, 2008). Lorden (1998) and Tull (2006) found that 50–60% of student affairs professionals exit the industry within the first five years. Multiple research studies identified job dissatisfaction, work environment issues, declining morale, and negative transitions from graduate school to professional life as the primary reasons for departure (Berwick, 1992; Boehman, 2007; Conley, 2001, Rosser, 2004; Rosser & Javinar, 2003). More specifically, Marshall,

Gardner, Hughes, and Lowery (2016) explained dissatisfaction with role ambiguity, role conflict, stress, job burnout, work load, and perceived opportunities for career advancement as primary concerns from former student affairs professionals.

Similarly, multiracial individuals, those who identify with two or more racial heritages (Root, 1992; Root & Kelley, 2003), experience a variety of personal challenges related to acceptance, belonging, and self-esteem (Root, 1992). Yet, Sands and Schuh (2004) explained that these individuals developed coping mechanisms such as the ability to easily navigate in and out of social groups, evaluate systems to maximize benefits. They persevere as a result of perceived or actual isolation from peers, despite these challenges (Spicer-Runnels, 2015).

IMPOSTER PHENOMENON AND
ADMINISTRATORS OF COLOR

As the community of student affairs professionals, especially administrators, has become more diverse, the imposter phenomenon as well as characteristics of personal identity directly impact the way in which people lead and create change on campuses. As a Black and Puerto Rican professional whose career began as a 21-year-old director, advanced to an assistant vice presidency by age 29, and earned a master's in business administration and doctorate by age 27, I have been challenged and enriched primarily by experiences related to my age, race, or gender. Early in my career, I recognized that regardless of my competence, education, and experience, I would always be the youngest person in the room that often resulted in an immediate lack of respect. In those moments, it was difficult to distinguish what were actual forms of unfair treatment versus negative perceptions due to my lack of confidence. However, through professional advancement, mentorship, and maturity, it has become easier to differentiate circumstances and the best methods of response.

To navigate these experiences, I relied on lessons I learned as a multiracial child including leveraging my identities to navigate systems, exercising my ability to move in and out of subgroups, and applying an unwavering commitment to becoming my best self. I learned early in life how to assess and evaluate systems to determine the most efficient way to reach my goal. I developed and refined my ability to read my environment and calibrate my personal brand to enhance collaborative partnerships related to duties. Finally, I navigated imposter phenomenon battles internally to ensure that I privately overcame barriers that prevented me from moving towards my goals.

STRATEGIES TO OVERCOME IMPOSTER PHENOMENON

As the student affairs industry becomes more diverse and enriched by professionals that are qualified and have opportunities to advance, feelings of inadequacy do not disappear. The foundation of the student affairs profession is grounded in helping people become the best version of themselves and the imposter phenomenon can prevent individuals from reaching their potential. As people of color continue to populate institutions where they've been historically underrepresented and marginalized, I believe they must find ways to make systemic and personal changes that impact others regardless of their identity. For me, the strategy to creating these systemic and personal changes was guided by lessons learned through my multiracial identity: Learn the rules and change the game from within. As a multiracial person, I've always been comfortable engaging and adapting to new groups. This skill set helped me quickly understand the culture of subgroups within the campus community and how to leverage their influence.

Student affairs professionals of color should have an unquenchable thirst for knowledge about the inner workings of their institution. Too often, the desire to learn and advance remains within functional areas or divisions; but, the ability to understand and articulate how various functions of the institution integrate and advance the mission are invaluable. Professionals of color should not become victims of self-imposed limitations due to traditional approaches of navigating and advancing within student affairs. The increase of professionals of color in student affairs, especially administrator roles, is a game changer and as a result, new rules may need to be applied. In my experience, these rules included actively building an academic portfolio that included teaching experience and publications, vocalizing power and authority as a content expert within my discipline and becoming more engaged in fundraising initiatives. Additionally, professionals of color can create positive change within their institutions by maximizing the influence of their positions and the campus partners. One of the best ways to overcome the imposter phenomenon is to take healthy calculated risks that increase self-perceived competency. For example, I volunteered to present the division's annual budget requests to the resource committee in response to our vice president's absence. This experience elevated my exposure on campus because these presentations are typically done by members of the president's cabinet and required that I understand every aspect of each budget I presented. I considered this opportunity a healthy risk because I knew my peers would be invested in my success since it contributed to their needs. In doing so, professionals of color model behavior that demonstrates how to create positive change and potentially provides courage to others. As professionals of color advance into administrator roles, there are countless opportunities to initiate change for the betterment of all people as well as advance a culture of excellence.

Transcending the imposter phenomenon takes inward and outward courage. Using strategies rooted in increasing comprehensive knowledge and taking calculated risks provides professionals of color the opportunity to remain anchored to their core values and beliefs while stretching their potential. In my experience, I recognized that knowledge acquisition was the best tool to help me overcome personal barriers placed by imposter phenomenon and lingering impacts of my multiracial identity. Intentionally seeking opportunities to diversify my skill set and knowledge base provided the opportunity to leverage characteristics associated with my multiracial identity. Characteristics, such as the ability to easily navigate in and out of groups and evaluate systems to maximize benefits, were instrumental in helping me advance while managing the interaction of my imposter feelings and multiracial identity. Furthermore, while some professionals within the division and beyond focus on becoming specialists, the ability to become a generalist and understand the inner workings of the institution can address imposter feelings, boost confidence, and increase professional value to the organization.

CONCLUSION

As my network has expanded, I've found that people of color are impacted by the imposter phenomenon differently; regardless, many have developed strategies to assist with coping, thriving, and redirecting their mind-sets. Professionals of color have historically repurposed barriers into opportunities and the imposter phenomenon has the potential to continue this tradition. While there is still a lot to learn, professionals of color will continue to reframe the impact of the imposter phenomenon and master the ability to use it as a tool to direct their professional growth and move closer towards becoming a better version of themselves.

REFERENCES

Berwick, K. R. (1992). Stress among student affairs administrators: The relationship of personal characteristics and organizational variables on work-related stress. *Journal of College Student Development, 33*(1), 11–19.

Boehman, J. (2007). Affective commitment among student affairs professionals. *NASPA Journal, 44*(2), 307–326. https://doi.org/10.2202/1949-6605.1797

Clance, P. R., & Imes, S. A. (1978). The imposter phenomenon in high achieving women: Dynamics and therapeutic intervention. *Psychotherapy: Theory, Research & Practice, 15*(3), 241–247. https://doi.org/10.1037/h0086006

Cokley, K., McClain, S., Enciso, A., & Martinez, M. (2013). An examination of the impact of minority status stress and impostor feelings on the mental health of diverse ethnic minority college students. *Journal of Multicultural Counseling and Development, 41,* 82–95. https://doi.org/10.1002/j.2161-1912.2013.00029.x

Conley, V. M. (2001). Separation: An integral aspect of the staffing process. *College Student Affairs Journal, 21*(1), 57–63.

Cowman, S., & Ferrari, J. (2002). "Am I for real?" Predicting impostor tendencies from self-handicapping and affective components. *Social Behavior and Personality: An international journal, 30,* 119–126. https://doi.org/10.2224/sbp.2002.30.2.119

Gibson-Beverly, G., & Schwartz, J. P. (2008). Attachment, entitlement and the impostor phenomenon in female graduate students. *Journal of College Counseling, 11*(2008), 119–132.

Hutchins, H. M. (2015), Outing the imposter: A study exploring imposter phenomenon among higher education faculty. *New Horizons in Adult Education and Human Resource Development, 27,* 3–12. https://doi.org/10.1002/nha3.20098

Lorden, L. (1998). Attrition in the student affairs profession. *NASPA Journal, 35*(3), 207–216. https://doi.org/10.2202/1949-6605.1049

Marshall, S. M., Gardner, M. M., Hughes, C., & Lowery, U. (2016). Attrition from student affairs: Perspectives from those who exited the profession. *Journal of Student Affairs Research and Practice, 53*(2), 146–159. https://doi.org/10.1080/19496591.2016.1147359

Renn, K. A., & Jessup-Anger, E. R. (2008). Preparing new professionals: Lessons for graduate preparation programs from the national study of new professionals in student affairs. *Journal of College Student Development, 49*(4), 319–335. https://doi.org/10.1353/csd.0.0022

Root, M. P. (1992). *Racially mixed people in America.* Newbury Park, CA: SAGE.

Root, M. P., & Kelley, M. (2003). *The Multiracial Child Resource Book.* Seattle, WA: Mavin Foundation.

Rosser, V. J. (2004). A national study on midlevel leaders in higher education: The unsung professionals in the academy. *Higher Education, 48*(3), 317–337. https://doi.org/10.1023/B:HIGH.0000035543.58672.52

Rosser, V. J., & Javinar, J. M. (2003). Midlevel student affairs leaders' intentions to leave: Examining the quality of their professional and institutional work life. *Journal of College Student Development, 44*(6), 813–830. https://doi.org/10.1353/csd.2003.0076

Sands, N., & Schuh, J. H. (2004). Identifying interventions to improve the retention of biracial students: A case study. *Journal of College Student Retention, 5*(4), 349–363. https://doi.org/10.2190/QT6X-MH0T-EAKJ-U6RF

Spicer-Runnels, A. D. (2015). High school to college transition: An examination of the influence of social and academic integration on multiracial college student persistence. In T. Hicks & C. W. Lewis (Eds.), *High school to college transition research studies* (pp. 129–152). Lanham, MA: University Press of America.

Tull, A. (2006). Synergistic supervision, job satisfaction, and intention to turn over of new professionals in student affairs. *Journal of College Student Development, 47*(4), 465–480. https://doi.org/10.1353/csd.2006.0053

CHAPTER 17

SCRATCHING AND SURVIVING IN RESIDENTIAL LIFE

Good Times

Aaron Slocum
Indiana State University

Individuals of color who work in housing may face many different challenges because of their supervisor's lack of knowledge, information, experience, understanding, and failure to be relatable. Blacks often find themselves as one of a few people of color who works in residential life. These challenges can be negated if there is space to share and pass information. I will draw from my experiences and provide tips and techniques that advanced my career and set me aside from my peers. This chapter will discuss red flags, Black secrets to propel your career, how to be the housing employee everyone loves, and recommendations for working in an unwelcoming environment.

I was born and raised in Milwaukee, Wisconsin, a city known for poverty, violence, police brutality, and racial discrimination amongst its Black

No Ways Tired, pages 157–164
Copyright © 2019 by Information Age Publishing

citizens (Boulton, 2014; Downs, 2015). Educational attainment and career advancement are hard for many Black youth from impoverished communities (Cameron & Heckman, 2001). The lack of resources and jobs make it tough for individuals to break the poverty cycle (Connell, 1994). As a young man from this area, I was determined to do something better with my life. I graduated from high school and pursued my bachelor's degree at the University of Wisconsin-Parkside (UW-P), which is located 45 minutes southeast of Milwaukee. As a student at UW-P, for the first time, I felt free from Milwaukee's inner city struggles and I began to develop into a young leader. I started my student leadership in housing as a resident assistant (RA) during my sophomore year and continued until I graduated. As an RA, I interacted with students through programming, listening to their concerns, and helping many students of color navigate college, graduate, and become productive citizens. During my time as an RA, I had several student affairs mentors who encouraged me to enroll in graduate school. Like many individuals who find themselves in student affairs, it was my mentors who exposed me to the field and told me about the opportunity to attend graduate school for free. I listened to their advice and applied to schools across the country.

I was accepted into a graduate program at Lake View University (LVU), where I pursued a master's degree in student affairs and higher education. I chose an assistantship within the department of residential life, because I was familiar with the working environment. This assistantship was beneficial because I did not have to pay for housing, food, or tuition and I was offered a monthly stipend. While working as an assistant hall director at LVU, I realized I was isolated. I was the only Black male working in housing and in my cohort, which was a shock for me. Not only was I the only Black male in my department, but the city also did not have businesses that catered to individuals of color, which varied significantly from Milwaukee, Wisconsin. For example, it was difficult finding a Black church, barber, and ethnic foods. I quickly realized my time at LVU was going to be challenging. I had to not only learn how to survive, but also how to thrive in this atmosphere. Growing up in Milwaukee, my mother preached education was the way out of poverty and the fear of not wanting to be a failure, along with my upbringing, taught me that failure was not an option.

Lake View University has a large population of minority undergraduate students and as a graduate student in residential life, most of my interactions were with undergraduate students. The Black student body received me well and I began developing connections with students and encouraging them to succeed and pursue graduate school. I was often invited to Black-focused programs and often approached by students who sought to transfer to my staff or begged me to hire them as my front desk or student staff worker. The unfortunate part about being the only Black male working in housing is that I found myself overextended. While the students provided me access to the Black community, I was not experiencing it in my cohort, department, or the community. I found myself drained. Students and staff wanted me to serve as their mentor and attend programs while also balancing both my job and graduate school responsibilities. Although I found myself fatigued, I knew the important role I fulfilled through my student interactions and in those moments with my staff. Students seemed thirsty for Black attention and I had to give them the same energy they were giving me. In the 2 years I worked as a graduate student in housing, I made several connections with Black students and watched many of them pursue graduate degrees. However, I quickly learned many predominantly White institutions do not hire many Black men and women in administrative roles. This lack of diversity on college campuses create extra work for the small pockets of faculty and staff of color (Kayes, 2006).

After completing my graduate studies at LVU, I began my professional journey at Valley State University (VSU) as a full-time hall director. VSU is a state school, the institution felt like a private institution. The students were privileged and many knew all they had to do to resolve an issue was to have one of their parents call the Department of Residence Life. The privilege of the students and their parents did not sit well with me. Many of the non-majority students would overlook faculty and staff of color and there were instances of microaggressions in which a student would think I was a custodian, maintenance worker, or a coach on one of the athletic teams.

My time at VSU did not last long and there were several factors that contributed to me leaving and seeking employment closer to home—micromanaging, feeling I was not fully using my talents, lack of opportunity for advancement, and my brother's health issues. I spent 11 months at VSU before returning to my alma mater as an area coordinator with the Office of Residential Life at LVU.

While there were several benefits related to my return to LVU, the grass was not greener on the other side. I frequently found myself working long hours without recognition, competing for resources, and dealing with incompetent supervisors, multiple leadership changes, and poor communication. These issues affected work output, team morale, and employee mental health. In addition, LVU struggles with retaining students of color. Every semester I witnessed students leaving mid-semester. Some of the factors that caused college students to leave were financial issues, unwelcoming environments, academic unpreparedness, and social isolation (Thayer, 2000; Warburton, Bugarin, & Nunez, 2001). As a staff member, the number of students of color seeking my assistance increased and I found myself helping more and more individuals of color. The students I helped were so surprised by the personal attention and concern they received that they began telling others to come see me. It became overwhelming and I had to stop. I questioned how to resolve my racial battle fatigue (RBF)—experienced by African Americans and other marginalized and stigmatized groups who due to extreme and consistent racial discrimination, microaggressions, and bigotry (Smith, 2004)—but also provide the students with the resources and guidance they needed since there was a lack of Black male professionals and university support for students of color. The solution for me was to create two living-learning communities for young men and women of color in which I provided participants with a team of professionals on campus to support them and create an atmosphere where students could lean on one another to excel academically and socially on campus.

While in the process of securing resources to establish the living-learning communities, I was accepted to the educational leadership doctoral program. On my first day of class for my doctoral program, a leadership team member approached me and said, "You are not going to be able to skate your way through this one." Believe it or not, this statement did not catch me off guard since I witnessed a reaction of jealousy from this same individual when I made the announcement that I was accepted to the doctoral program. Her statement confirmed that she was not going to be supportive of my PhD pursuit. From that moment on, I felt constant pressure and unacceptable scrutiny. I was questioned about my whereabouts, how I was spending my time, what I was doing with my staff, and received unannounced check-ups during my office hours. These behaviors were annoying because none of my peers received the same scrutiny. I knew my time in residential life was coming to an end as I was increasingly overwhelmed with the stress of working a 24/7 job, the lack of diversity, and inconsistencies with the treatment of employees. My happiness and personal wellness will always be more important than a job.

BLACK SECRETS THAT WILL PROPEL YOUR CAREER

My time in residential life taught me a lot about politics, student affairs, and myself. My personal experiences working in residential life helped me pinpoint critical characteristics that individuals of color must have to survive in university housing. The following information details what I perceive as keys to success for entry-level and mid-level professionals of color to equip themselves with skills to maneuver through residential life, which no one shared with me but ultimately allowed me to excel in residential life.

Preparation and Preservation

Housing employers love employees who never stop learning and become scholars of the field. The key to becoming a scholar of the field is staying involved and active by attending and presenting at conferences, educating your peers and coworkers, remaining knowledgeable about things going on at different institutions and watching for trends occurring in housing. Learning how to be a team player is directly related to setting trends and entails working together with other employees to get a task or assignment completed, stepping up when needed, and contributing ideas and information when it is appropriate.

Furthermore, having a career plan will make it easier to advance and will prevent you from staying in the same position for an overextended period of time. Many housing professionals become stagnant in their career by staying in the same position at the same institution for years. Find ways to be invested in your personal career growth and development, seeking opportunities to build skills and experiences that will help you move into your next position.

Do Not Be Afraid

There is a continual search within student affairs for new innovative ideas. One cannot be afraid to rock the boat and try something new. You want to challenge the system as you rock the boat, while simultaneously being cautious about picking your battles wisely. Consider what is essential and worth challenging. Also, do not be afraid to advocate for yourself and others. As an individual working in university housing, you will face challenges, but it is important to always keep your best interest at the forefront. Lastly, do not be afraid to take on challenging tasks, create something, or go above and beyond to stand out among your peers. Even if you fail at something, you are learning what to do and what not to do for the next time.

Learn the Art of Storytelling

Mastering the art of storytelling involves creating an emotional connection with the listeners and encouraging change (Simmons, 2006). Stories can focus on your personal life, work and situation you handled. The skilled housing employee will use the art of storytelling sparingly to help others understand and grasp various lessons. As a housing professional, stories can advance your career by allowing you to become a memorable and relatable.

Move in Silence

Moving in silence is important to the success of housing professionals, specifically because they work, live, and interact with people often in the same space each day. This arrangement can be very hard for some individuals with the existence of social media platforms and the personal desire to publicly show the work they are doing through pictures and captions. While publicizing your work successes is acceptable, sometimes it is good to express humility and do things without the world knowing. When you move in silence with your ideas, it also reduces the chances of someone stealing them. Additionally, it prevents the jealousy that may come from different co-workers. Moving in silence allows for a greater appreciation of your work and it shows others that you can be efficient in taking on more while staying on top of your daily responsibilities.

Always Smile

It is important to realize the impact a genuine smile can have. Smiling at work can open doors and opportunities for you. Sometimes when we smile, even when we do not want to, it has the ability to change both our perspective and others' and can result in someone getting needed resources or additional assistance. Individuals like to work and collaborate with colleagues who they perceive to have a kind-hearted spirit. However, if you are unhappy, do not be afraid to show your displeasure.

Navigate Politics

Being savvy and aware of politics can play a significant role in the success of an individual and how far they will go. Unfortunately, in the university housing setting as in most units in higher education, politics have great influence. As an employee, you should learn how to be aware of and properly play the political game. If you fail to learn about politics, you may potentially get passed up for promotions, unique opportunities, much needed resources, and support. Play the game but be careful. When it comes to department politics, three rules have guided me throughout my career— learn the organizational structure and pinpoint the key players within the organization/ department who can inform you about whom is in charge as well as strengths and weaknesses when it comes to leadership and mobility; strategically build a network of colleagues in your department and in the campus community that will provide you information, collaborate with you on projects, and provide you support; and never sell your soul because if something goes against your morals and beliefs, it is imperative you stand up for yourself and speak your mind while remaining mindful of wording, tone, and the future.

Understanding Perception Is Everything

It is crucial for you to make sure you represent yourself well, especially if your department does not have a favorable reputation. You cannot hide the office you work for, but you can separate yourself and your work ethic from the department by creating a unique reputation. Furthermore, as an individual of color, everything you do will be evaluated (i.e., the way you communicate, dress, interact, work ethic, and your ability to get a task done efficiently). You must remember someone is always observing how you perform.

Be Yourself—The Good and the Bad

The last suggestion I recommend for advancing your career is to be yourself while also being mindful of how you interact with your colleagues. Being your true self can create happiness for yourself and others and create a personal connection with colleagues and students but be careful of the information you share. In contrast, they will sniff out a phony persona. So, do not be afraid to be yourself at all times, on good and bad days.

RECOMMENDATIONS ON HOW TO EXIST IN AN UNWELCOMING ENVIRONMENT

To survive as an individual of color in an unwelcoming environment, it is imperative for you to build a network outside of residential life. It is important to make sure you network wisely; accordingly, find a trustworthy individual who will listen to you and provide sound advice when needed. Also, remember to document all negative problematic encounters, whether in-person, via email, or phone. Lastly, if things do not improve, hopefully you will realize that your happiness and sanity are more important than a job. Finding a place where you feel accepted and welcomed and a position that is better aligned with your values are important.

REFERENCES

Boulton, G. (2014, September 10). Wisconsin Black children remain trapped in poverty, study says. *The Milwaukee Journal Sentinel.* Retrieved from http://archive.jsonline.com/business/wisconsins-black-children-remain-trapped-in-poverty-study-says-b99348240z1-274562101.html/

Cameron, S. V., & Heckman, J. J. (2001). The dynamics of educational attainment for Black, Hispanic, and White males. *Journal of Political Economy, 109*(3), 455–499.

Connell, R. (1994). Poverty and education. *Harvard Educational Review, 64*(2), 125–150.

Downs, K. (2015, March 5). Why is Milwaukee so bad for Black people? Code switch race and identity, remix. *National Public Radio.* Retrieved from http://www.npr.org/sections/codeswitch/2015/03/05/390723644/why-is-milwaukee-so-bad-for-black-people

Kayes, P. E. (2006). New paradigms for diversifying faculty and staff in higher education: Uncovering cultural biases in the search and hiring process. *Multicultural Education, 14*(2), 65–69.

Simmons, A. (2006). *The story factor: Inspiration, influence, and persuasion through the art of storytelling.* New York, NY: Basic Books.

Smith, W. A. (2004). Black faculty coping with racial battle fatigue: The campus racial climate in a post-civil rights era. *A long way to go: Conversations about race by African American faculty and graduate students, 14,* 171–190.

Thayer, P. B. (2000, May). Retention of students from first generation and low-income backgrounds. *The Opportunity Outlook: Council for Opportunity in Education,* 2–9.

Warburton, E. C., Bugarin, R., & Nunez, A. M. (2001). *Bridging the gap: Academic preparation and postsecondary success of first-generation students.* Statistical Analysis Report, National Center for Education Statistics. Retrieved from https://nces.ed.gov/pubs2001/2001153.pdf

CHAPTER 18

CRITNOIR

Naming and Claiming the Reality of Anti-Blackness in Student Affairs

Terah J. Stewart
Iowa State University

Joan Collier
Rutgers University

Marvette Lacy
University of Wisconsin–Milwaukee

Recently, higher education and student affairs educators have been engaged in conversations about racism and White supremacy in meaningful and material ways. Through this chapter, we suggest that conversations around anti-Black racism are either peripheral to or simply nonexistent in the student affairs racism discourse. We offer a story from a mid-level administrator who had to manage anti-Black sentiments and behavior from student affairs professionals of color (POCs). In addition, we offer our musings on the implications of anti-Black ideas and beliefs. Conceptual considerations for a critical framework that centers the pervasiveness of anti-Blackness and its implications for student affairs are suggested along with strategies to persist.

No Ways Tired, pages 165–175
Copyright © 2019 by Information Age Publishing

Racism and White supremacy will continue to be an ongoing conversation within the context of research and practitioner work in student affairs, but we must dig deeper to discuss how these oppressions show up in ways that give nuance to other types of ignorance and bigotry. One of these manifestations is through anti-Black racism, which we will interchangeably refer to as anti-Blackness in this chapter. While the concept of anti-Blackness is not new, the way we will position and discuss it will be slightly different than how some of the literature portrays it. Typically, anti-Blackness is utilized as a concept to discuss the ways White people and the dominant gaze perpetuates oppression toward the lives and experiences of Black people (Black Americans to be specific) as opposed to how they oppress other people of color in both historical and contemporary contexts (Douglas, 2017; Nighaoui, 2017; Stein, 2016). However, our experiences and discussion will face a different direction that deepens the conversation to include all the ways people of color also collude with anti-Black oppressions. Next, we will briefly discuss, explain, and problematize critical race theory in an effort to situate the discussions of our experiences and as means to create space for this issue within the discourse.

CRITICAL RACE THEORY

Critical race theory (CRT) began as a framework connected to critical legal studies and was intended to serve as a legal reframe to examine the prevalence of racism in the justice system. Over time, scholars have used CRT as a critical framework that highlights the normalcy and pervasiveness of racism in almost every facet of American life (Delgado & Stefancic, 2012). Since its introduction into the legal discourse, scholars of various disciplines have used CRT to examine how race and racism manifest in social, cultural, and academic contexts, resulting in the development of other critical studies (Mueller, 2013; Patton, 2016; Salter & Adams, 2013; Wing, 1997).

Numerous scholars and educators have utilized CRT to branch out and generate other critical perspectives and theories, many of which include important considerations of the sociocultural factors in the lives of people of color. For example, tribal critical scholarship offers a deep focus on colonization as central to understanding and deconstructing the experiences of Indigenous peoples in the United States (Brayboy, 2005). Asian critical scholarship includes interrogation of cultural aspects such as how Asian stereotypes affect members of the community as well as a focus on transnational contexts that are significant to understanding and engaging their experiences (Museus & Iftikar, 2013). Critical scholarship continues to grow across disciplines and identity groups, including disability (DisCrit), multiracial theory (MultiracialCrit), and Latinx communities (LatCrit; An-namma, Connor, & Ferri, 2016; Harris, 2016; Valdes, 1998).

Scholars have critiqued CRT for its exceptionalism of African American histories and legacies in the United States as well as a problematization of the Black–White binary as being limiting to other racial minority groups and their experiences (Delgado & Stefancic, 2012). Given all that we know about racecrits, we offer one simple question: Where is BlackCrit, specifically? While we have been unable to locate where the following has been claimed explicitly in the literature, it *seems* to be that many scholars and researchers consider CRT a framework that frames the Black experience within the critical discourse. We find it problematic because if CRT as a framework is supposed to represent what BlackCrit could be or what it could mean, it is lacking some depth and nuance. To be clear, we recognize the vast body of research and literature about Black people and the Black experience, but in our view, they do not seem to be viewed, used, or positioned collectively in the crit theory discourse to bring about discussion specifically on anti-Blackness from other communities of color *in addition to* White people.

HYPERVISIBLE

As an assistant director of a multicultural center, I (TJ) was familiar with the work of creating supportive and affirming environments for students within the context of predominantly White institutions (PWIs) and the system of dominance they often perpetuate. When I began my role, I took comfort in knowing (and hoping) that my colleagues, like me, understood the odds we and our students faced. I hoped that we were all committed to equity and justice and that we would welcome the challenging aspects of the tiresome but most important work. Our center employed staff members with responsibilities for education, programming, and support of the Latino, LGBTQ, Indigenous, Asian/Asian American, African/African-American, and women communities on campus. There was one professional staff member dedicated to each of these communities and they all were part of my team. I was one of three assistant directors and we all reported to an executive director.

During my time in that role, I was honored to report to a Black woman in a division overseen by a Black woman (vice-president of student affairs) who sat on a cabinet with a Black woman (vice-provost for diversity & inclusion/outreach and engagement), all under the tutelage of a Black university president. Surely, given the history of White supremacy and the traditional exclusion of minortized individuals from leadership opportunities, I believed their presence in these roles should be celebrated by all. Within the context of our institution, I believed we had taken great steps toward being inclusive in our hiring practices. However, I did not realize that in some ways the visibility of these particular leaders would feed into the very real problem of hypervisibility that Black people have faced throughout history (Browne, 2015; Mowatt, French, & Malebranche, 2013) and at that time on our campus.

During one-on-one meetings with my staff members, I liked to spend our time discussing challenges, successes, student concerns, and any progress on their work. Increasingly those foci were derailed and switched to interrogations of their perceptions regarding unbalanced (over) support toward African American student initiatives which, quite frankly, was confusing and alarming to me. I received questions from my non-Black POC staff and had to explain how and why Black students and programs seemed to get "so much" at our institutions in comparison to other constituency groups that we serve. I regularly had to field questions about why the staff of the Black cultural center collaborated so regularly with our own Black student programs and less with other racial identity programs. I had to field questions about their perceptions of the lack of engagement by Black senior administrators with their constituency programs as opposed to administrators' involvement in Black student programs. I had to field questions about my *own* engagement with programs and if I believed the needs of Black students and the Black community deserved to be privileged. To be clear, I believe that one's perception is reality and unfortunately, sometimes that perception is an anti-Black one.

As an administrator, it was important to me that my time and our resources were equitable among all of our staff and constituency groups. I believed that I achieved that balance in equity (not equality) and soon, I gave up on trying to appease my non-Black POC staff and focus on how we could better support all of our students. I gave up on trying to convince them as I believed my energy could be better spent on working with our non-Black students of color to make sure they were getting what they needed from our center. One day, I attended a meeting with some student leaders and I will always remember the exact moment that I checked out of the conversation. It was when one of the students stated, "I just think it is really unfair that Black students have their own cultural center (academic affairs) and support from an Intercultural Specialist (student affairs) when the rest of us only have one." That comment was one of many that expressed anti-Black sentiments and while I have significantly more patience and understanding with students and their learning and growth, it was not any less disappointing to learn that comment reflected how many of the non-Black students of color felt.

LOOKING BACK

The problem with the questions from the non-Black POC staff and their subsequent beliefs was that they were all unknowingly focusing their frustration (some of them valid) on questioning the work, progress, and community around Black issues and not the pervasive Whiteness and White supremacy on campus. Dominance constructs conditions in such a way that it will often make POC *feel* like we are in competition with one another. That type of energy is counterproductive to equity and justice and instead, our efforts must focus on coalition building and disrupting real and true dominance where it exists. The fact that I was often asked to speak for the behavior or decisions by other Black staff was also, to me, wildly inappropriate.

The very questions that were asked, side-comments that were made, and negative energy that was projected were deeply rooted in their own anti-Black attitudes. Their beliefs were similar to many anti-Black conversations such as "Why are the needs and concerns of Black people always centered?"; "Why is #BlackLivesMatter *always* the topic of conversation?"; and "Why are Black people heard and catered to before other marginalized identity groups?" What they seemed to be picking up on is the very real issue of the hypervisibility of Blackness (Browne, 2015). The problem with those "questions" and their limited perspectives is that they ignored all the ways Black people experience violence, erasure, and hurdles as a result of hypervisibility. There also seemed to be a constant desire for the labor and resources of Black staff, students, and administrators (for their constituent community issues and concerns) with no offering of their own labor, which too is a form of anti-Blackness.

As for our students, I do not expect them to know all of the politics and intricacies of university governance. I had hoped that some of what I was experiencing with my staff and their attitudes about the support of Black people and students at our university was unique to them; it was not. Non-Black SOC were harboring some of the same attitudes and beliefs. It was hard to know that any ground gained toward the support of the Black community at our large PWIs was/would often be criticized or questioned if it was not also offered to other non-Black minoritized groups, even if those things achieved were a result of the hard work and labor of those Black students and Black professionals.

To be clear, I did not/do not think that the matter of available resources, the equity of their distribution, and the "representation" of race among leadership was ever beyond reproach. However, any immediate and relentless reaction to Black progress as a criticism of their achievements and the space they take up, *instead* of criticisms on White supremacy and the space it takes up illustrates anti-Black sentiments in practice. It would be more productive to acknowledge all the ways Black people have been historically unrepresented/misrepresented and excluded and highlight how White supremacy in all of its violence positions communities of color and other marginalized entities to feel like we are competing for limited resources. The space that *Whiteness* and White people take up is the problem, *not* the "scraps" that Black people have fought for and occasionally receive.

INTRODUCING CRITNOIR

We offer CritNoir as a new concept within the critical discourse that aims to highlight the pervasiveness of anti-Black sentiments and praxis within everyday life. Specifically, we argue that the reality of anti-Blackness is not simply related to the ways that White people uniquely oppress Black people, but that there is a universal disdain and subjugation of Blackness and Black people that is maintained and perpetuated by everyone, including other Black people at times.

Among other things, CritNoir is a way of thinking that critically considers and notices when values, attitudes, beliefs, and their praxis enact forms of oppression, violence, and erasure specifically toward and about Black people, their experiences, expressions, histories, legacies, and values. It is important to reflect, recognize, and correct these sentiments to ensure we are not engendering harm on Black people who we live and work with every day.

By introducing this concept, we are not suggesting that Black people are unable to engage in the perpetuation of oppressions, dominance, or inequitable practices; on the contrary, any person, regardless of identity, is able to perpetuate dominance, particularly from their privileged identity spaces. To this end, within the context of CritNoir, we also boldly assert that Black people can be, and often are, complicit in anti-Blackness, which reflects the pervasive nature of anti-Black violence, attitudes, and behavior(s). Anti-Blackness can and does function in the absence of Whiteness *because* of White supremacy. While we reject the notion of a Black–White binary, Blackness is diametrically opposed to Whiteness on a Black–White continuum.

(UN)LEARNING ANTI-BLACKNESS

While there are global/universal implications for this type of oppression that is comfortably located within the larger system of dominance, we will focus on considerations and discussion of this concept specifically within the context of student affairs. Furthermore, where and when someone might wield decision-making power and influence, they should use that power to create meaningful dialogue opportunities and policy changes toward creating equity for all minoritized groups and constituencies.

In addition, for non-Black colleagues of color, unlearning means you must be willing abandon anti-Black ideals and sentiments and to focus energy toward critiquing White supremacy as the basis for the collective of negative experiences. Disrupting White supremacy is a more powerful coalition-building strategy than unfairly critiquing the space that Blackness takes up.

Unlearning the anti-Blackness that permeates institutional culture and everyday practices is a journey. Moving toward liberation requires thoughtful, deliberate, and disciplined work. Critical literature is a great tool that offers critiques of systems instead of critiques of people, as such we urge everyone to (re)consider and (re)imagine their ideas related to how we encourage, correct, and support Black students and colleagues.

STRATEGIES TO PERSIST

We recognize that dealing with anti-Black racism is not a new phenomenon and will likely persist for many years to come as we continue to struggle for freedom from the system of dominance. Below we have listed five strategies that we have personally used to help mitigate difficult experiences during our multiple tenures in student affairs roles. Our experiences have been varied and have transcended from entry level, mid-level, and faculty roles with various supervisory experiences. We recommend engaging any given recommendation based on your level of comfort and influence. Lastly, we recommend self-care and self-preservation, recognizing it also as an act of radical resistance.

Learning to (Un)learn

> *Education is the most powerful weapon which you can use to change the world.*
> —Nelson Mandela (https://www.brainyquote.com/quotes/
> nelson_mandela_157855)

Spend time engaging critical texts (both peer reviewed and conceptual) to help you learn more about exactly *what* you are experiencing. This process is important because the more literature you consume, the better you are able to articulate when anti-Black sentiment and practice show up in your work and experience. Learning about these concepts will also be important for engaging in the work of deconstructing your own anti-Black attitudes and proclivities, if they exist. Finally, some of the best writing and work available on topics of privilege, oppression, and anti-Black racism are written by unaffiliated Black women, queer, and trans folk on blogs and social media platforms.

Cultivate Community

It's not the load that breaks you down, it's the way you carry it.

—Lena Horne (https://www.goodreads.com/quotes/314889-it-s-not -the-load-that-breaks-you-down-it-s-the)

The importance of cultivating community as part of persisting in student affairs cannot be overstated. The work we attempt to do is difficult. None of us should ever have to move on this path alone, particularly when experiencing issues around anti-Black behavior and sentiments. Community manifests in different ways for each of us. For some, it may mean joining a Black faculty/staff alliance or resource group. For others, it may mean finding a colleague to share a biweekly lunch or coffee meeting to simply vent and process the frustrations you are experiencing in your office and through your work. Explore what works for you and try to seek out that strategy. Finally, remember that the best way to cultivate community is to show yourself to be supportive of others.

Call Out to Call In

". . . when we speak we are afraid our words will not be heard nor welcomed but when we are silent we are still afraid. So, it is better to speak."

—Audre Lorde, A Litany of Survival (1978, p. 31)

When you experience non-Black colleagues of color engaging in anti-Black politics and behavior, call it out. Audre Lorde (1983) reminds us that there is no hierarchy of oppressions and as such, it is important to remember our liberation is tied to others'. No one can do the work alone. Colleagues can be a great source of support if you can help them learn and redirect their anger/frustration/critique to the system of White supremacy and dominance. Ultimately, if you can call them *in*, you will have more support for the next challenge that you encounter in your student affairs journey. To be clear, if the person or entity occupies a space of both professional and identity-based power, it will likely be difficult to call them/it out without consequences to that call out. Make choices based on what is best for you and your situation and remember that without conflict, there is no change.

Rest

Caring for myself is not self-indulgence, it is self-preservation,
and that is an act of political warfare.
—Audre Lorde, *A Burst of Light: And Other Essays* (1988, p. 130)

We so often push and work to resist oppressive environments and struc-tures that we sometimes forget to pause, reflect, and rest. We recognize that self-care and balance will manifest differently for each person and simply advocate for taking time to rest and engage in things that bring you hap-piness and joy. No single person will eradicate the prevalence of anti-Black attitudes and their consequences in one day or even one lifetime; there-fore, denying yourself comfort and joy is not in and of itself antithetical to the work of equity and justice. So, take time off if you can and take mental health days when you need them (and if allowed).

Exit

The price one pays for pursuing any profession, or calling,
is an intimate knowledge of its ugly side.
—James Baldwin, *The Price of the Ticket: Collected Nonfiction, 1948–1985*
(1985, p. 302)

Perhaps the most important strategy we can offer is being honest with yourself and know when it is time to make your exit from a toxic work en-vironment, particularly when you have exhausted all other strategies. We each make decisions about where to apply for professional opportunities for very specific and personal reasons. We also realize that those same per-sonal contexts can, and often do, inform how long we stay in a certain role or environment. We recommend making realistic decisions about when leaving is the best course of action for your situation. Sometimes, the best thing you can do is remove yourself and try to find a more welcoming and affirming environment that can support and appreciate your talents.

CONCLUSION

CritNoir and its various implications will be vital toward future endeavors of fostering a more inclusive student affairs profession; one that will allow the professionals of color to both survive and thrive. Far too often, excep-tionally talented people have departed from the important work of student affairs, student development, and higher education administration as a result of toxic and violent environmental contexts.

Although we only presented one story as part of our explanation of how anti-Blackness manifests in student affairs, through our experiences and observations we know that there are countless other stories and experiences. Anti-Blackness is manifested in each dress code policy that polices our hair, clothing, and the way we speak. Anti-Blackness is revealed when our knowledge and experiences come into question as being real and legitimate. Anti-Blackness is perpetuated in each moment that our labor is exploited, co-opted, unappreciated, or erased. We know these realities because we live them every day, both in and out of student affairs.

As a nation, we will have to contend with the complexities and consequences of the ongoing manifestations of White supremacy in our lives. One part of that recognition must include how anti-Black racism is connected to the very foundations of dominance and how we all collude in its proliferation. Anti-Blackness is a strong root that holds the system of dominance in place and if ignored, will ensure that the legacy of racism and White supremacy lives on forever.

REFERENCES

Annamma, S., Connor, D., & Ferri, B. (2016). Dis/ability critical race studies (Dis-Crit): Theorizing at the intersections of race and dis/ability. *Race Ethnicity and Education, 16*(1), 1–31.

Brayboy, B. (2005). Toward a tribal critical race theory in education. *Urban Review, 37*(5), 425–446. https://doi.org/10.1007/s11256-005-0018-y

Browne, S. (2015). *Dark matters: On the surveillance of Blackness.* Durham, NC: Duke University Press.

Delgado, R., & Stefancic, J. (2012). *Critical race theory: An introduction* (2nd ed.). New York, NY: New York University Press.

Douglas, K. B. (2017). Stop the violence: Breaking the cycle of anti-Black violence. *Interpretation: A Journal of Bible & Theology, 71*(4), 398–407. http://doi.org/10.1177/0020964317716130

Harris, J. C. (2016). Toward a critical multiracial theory in education. *International Journal of Qualitative Studies in Education (QSE), 29*(6), 795–813.

Lorde, A. (1983). *Homophobia and education.* New York, NY: Council on Interracial Books for Children.

Mowatt, R. A., French, B. H., & Malebranche, D. A. (2013). Black/female/body hypervisibility and invisibility: A Black feminist augmentation of feminist leisure research. *Journal of Leisure Research, 45*(5), 644–660.

Mueller, J. C. (2013). Tracing family, teaching race: Critical race pedagogy in the millennial sociology classroom. *Teaching Sociology, 41*(2), 172–187. http://doi.org/10.1177/0092055X12455135

Museus, S. D., & Iftikar, J. (2014). Asian critical theory (AsianCrit). In M. Y. Danico & J. G. Golson (Eds.), *Asian American society*. Thousand Oaks, CA: SAGE.

Nighaoui, S. C. (2017). The color of post-ethnicity: the civic ideology and the persistence of anti-Black racism. *Journal of Gender, Race and Justice, 20*, 349–379.

Patton, L. D. (2016). Disrupting postsecondary prose: Toward a critical race theory of higher education. *Urban Education, 51*(3), 315–342.

Salter, P., & Adams, G. (2013). Toward a critical race psychology. *Social & Personality Psychology Compass, 7*(11), 781–793. https://doi.org/10.1111/spc3.12068

Stein, S. (2016). Universities, slavery, and the unthought of anti-Blackness. *Cultural Dynamics, 28*(2), 169–187. https://doi.org/10.1177/0921374016634379

Valdes, F. (1998). Under construction: LatCrit consciousness, community, and theory. *California Law Review, 85*(5), 1087–1142.

Wing, A. K. (1997). *Critical race feminism: A reader*. New York: New York University Press.

CHAPTER 19

OUR WORK IS POLITICAL

Insights From Asian American Student Affairs Educators

rita zhang
University of California, Berkeley

Jude Paul Matias Dizon
University of Southern California

In this chapter, the authors share how their experiences with racism as Asian American student affairs educators provided a foundation to re-envision diversity work as political and liberatory. Rather than conforming to the pressures of the dominant culture in higher education, the authors challenge Asian American student affairs educators to proactively advance social justice work. The chapter offers insights and alternative perspectives to student affairs.

RITA

My life purpose is inextricably rooted in my ancestors' dreams and sacrifices that culminated in my mother's immigration to the United States. At age 24, my mom left poverty in Southern China for a better future for herself

No Ways Tired, pages 177–184
Copyright © 2019 by Information Age Publishing
All rights of reproduction in any form reserved.

and her unborn children. As I grew up, I witnessed my mother diligently learn a new language, work physically laborious jobs, and make sense of home away from homeland. Because of the resilience of my family through the generations, I now have the immense privilege and opportunity to live not only in survival, but to fight for the liberation of myself and my communities. I believe that education is the vehicle towards social transformation. My journey in higher education has been deeply provoking for both its infinite possibilities towards freedom as well as its pitfalls in recreating oppressive cycles. Guided by ancestral wisdom and a fundamental belief in fighting for the collective liberation of all oppressed peoples, I find my work in higher education as important and political as ever.

JUDE

I grew up 30 miles southeast of San Francisco in Union City, California. As a Filipino immigrant, working-class family, my parents clocked in overtime at the post office while my brother and I made sure we fit in and behaved at school. Although my school district had a majority of students of color, I learned very little about myself and from where I came. I worked hard to memorize whatever teachers impressed were important. In high school, this meant mastering Euro-American history and literature in order to graduate. Once in college, ethnic studies courses and learning from student of color activists changed my life. Finally, my education was relevant beyond an exam. I was awakened to the ongoing marginalization of people like me and my family. A critical education empowers communities to act upon the world, rather than accept what is given. As a higher education practitioner and scholar, I remain committed to the ethnic studies mission of self-determination against mechanisms of assimilation and control that are pervasive in schools and other U.S. institutions.

SHARING OUR JOURNEY

We are two Asian American student activists turned higher education professionals. As children of working-class, immigrant parents from under-resourced neighborhoods, college never felt like a choice as much as it was a necessity towards upward social mobility. Subsequently, college campuses have long been places of tension for us. We stepped onto the University of California, Berkeley campus with the awareness we were admitted but not sure how we would adjust to a new culture and fulfill our families' expectations. College soon became a home of empowerment and a site of resistance as we found student of color activist spaces and ethnic studies.

Our own consciousness-raising journeys merged identity development and political activism. Our involvement in student of color-led recruitment and retention was grounded in a critique of unjust policies and administrative decisions. We were committed to making the university a space for our communities.

Now, 10 years later, we continue to draw on our transformative experiences in activism to fuel us in our student affairs practice. Throughout our journeys from students to professionals, we have pushed one another to stay critical of our practice, supported each other through difficult work challenges, and reminded each other of our purpose during moments of hopelessness. In this chapter, we share our stories and a liberatory vision for Asian American student affairs educators and diversity work in higher education. We endeavor to inspire Asian American practitioners, particularly those beginning in their careers, to view our student affairs work as deeply political and to understand that we each have a role in shaping higher education institutions as accessible, equitable, and empowering environments.

COMMUNITY LIBERATION

A main concern of student affairs is psychosocial development (American Council on Education, 1937; Jones & Stewart, 2016). In graduate school, we appreciated, but were dissatisfied by, racial identity development theories that were often the only ways in which race and racism were discussed within student affairs (Kim, 2012; Kodama, McEwen, Liang, & Lee, 2002). Racial identity development theories describe the stages Asian American students undergo to understand their race in the status quo of U.S. racism. Racial identity development theories do not include a larger political analysis of institutionalized racism and its effects on race-related experiences of people of color. Our own experiences transitioning into the student affairs profession forced us to confront the racism in our institutions that identity development theory alone could not resolve.

During rita's master's program, she experienced culture shock in her move to the east coast. While she viewed student affairs as a vehicle to infiltrate the system to make change from within, rita quickly became aware of the complex scope of such work. The move east was not only to a predominantly and hxstorically White institution but to a racially homogenous profession (the "x" here and later in this chapter is used to critique gendered language where men are often used as the root word, i.e., history or women; the "x" symbolizes gender inclusion within the terms used). For the first time, rita entered spaces as one of only a literal handful of student affairs educators of color. She was regularly surprised at how little knowledge her colleagues had of Asian American issues. rita experienced racial microaggressions often, such as being confused for the few other Asian American womxn on campus, despite being of different ethnic backgrounds. These experiences continually reminded rita that simply breaking the barrier and representing Asian Americans in the field was not enough to eradicate systemic racism.

Jude was similarly challenged in his first full-time staff position as the sole student affairs educator dedicated to Asian American student involvement. His position was created out of student activism and placed in a multicultural affairs unit in the division of student affairs. Jude was involved in committees focused on students of color and observed how his colleagues would never bring up Asian American student concerns. Without an institutionalized position, Asian American students would be excluded from university racial equity efforts. Yet, despite serving in the very position that was supposed to represent Asian American student issues, Jude struggled to advance meaningful racial equity discourse when he had to continually convince colleagues of the racial exclusion Asian American students experienced.

Through many phone calls with one another, we expressed our frustration with being the representative Asian American and diversity expert but not given enough institutional leverage to create systemic change. To get through those moments, we often had to remind ourselves of what being Asian American truly means. We grounded ourselves by remembering that the emergence of an Asian American identity in the political movements of the late sixties was "not centered on the aura of racial identity, but embraced fundamental questions of oppression and power... the main thrust was not one of seeking legitimacy and representation within American society but the larger goal of liberation" (Omatsu, 2010, p. 299). For students taking on the new political identity of Asian American, liberation meant:

> to simply function as human beings, to control our own lives... initially, following the myth of the American Dream, we worked to attend predominantly White institutions, but we learned through direct analysis that it is impossible for our people, so-called minorities, to function as human beings, in a racist society (statement of the Philippine-American Collegiate Endeavor. (Omatsu, 2010, p. 302)

Although these words were written over 40 years ago, research and our experiences as practitioners make clear how Asian Americans on college campuses continue to face dehumanizing conditions (Museus & Park, 2015). Our identities, which we share with our students, are racialized and political. We are visibly marked as other—invisible and inconsequential within the power structure of the university. Our work in multicultural affairs, often a product of Asian American student activism, is rooted in the struggle for liberation, for the humanity of our students. How can we empower students to value themselves and also shift the campus environment so our students can function as full human beings? Centering our work in liberation, not just representational diversity, is essential to combating racism at the institutionalized levels so that our campuses can be the empowering and safe spaces that we seek to create.

DOING THE COMMUNITY WORK WITHIN

We are careful not to romanticize community liberation and presume that because we are a community, we all must agree and we are all the same. Within the field of student affairs, we believe organized racial affinity spaces need to be expanded to intentionally embody intersectional theory and practice. Intersectionality requires that we view our identities as greater than the sums of all our parts, and we must address oppression at all interlocking levels to be free (Crenshaw, 1989). Asian American liberation cannot be possible without recognizing that we are diverse across ethnicity, gender, sexual orientation, class status, and more. As such, the power and privilege associated with multiple and intersectional identities also manifest and operate within our community. We challenge Asian American student affairs educators to hold ourselves accountable in ensuring that our community, whether on campus or in our national associations, is an inclusive and equitable space for all of our intersecting identities.

Naming and challenging oppressive practices within our community has not been easy. For rita, Asian American professional development spaces often emphasized the need to "climb the ladder" to achieve higher status jobs. During conferences, rita felt pressured to network with the handful of Asian American senior-level administrators and faculty. When she chose to make a lateral career move to be closer to home, colleagues cautioned her against potentially harming her career trajectory. Though rita feels proud when there are Asian Americans in high ranking positions, she questions if career advancement should be *the* anti-racist strategy that our community emphasizes. Where is the distinction between advocating for representation versus assimilating into the White individualist capitalist system? Have we gotten lost in colonized mind-sets and taken on the oppressor's values of hierarchy, meritocracy, and status? We argue that true community liberation must go beyond replicating the same class inequality in which only a few can be at the top. We must redefine a new widened notion of what Asian American success and leadership can look like in higher education.

Similarly, we must also be critical of our practice and role modeling when working with Asian American students. During Jude's first full-time position, the state he worked in held an election for tuition equality for undocumented students. Jude solicited the Filipino American student organization for support of a speaking event featuring Jose Antonio Vargas, an undocumented Filipino American advocate for immigration reform. The leadership decided not to support the event because of different perspectives among the students on immigration. They cited that they were a "cultural organization" and therefore, not suited to be involved with a politicized issue. As cultural student group advisors, we may be expected by our supervisors to simply plan cultural showcases and heritage months. We are averse to this apolitical lens of "culture" as it reduces our identities and issues to entertainment. In this example, Jude sought to integrate an intersectional lens in his work with students. Culture goes beyond geography or food and can include the wider experiences of Asian Americans impacted by systematic racism and unjust policies. We believe student affairs practitioners, regardless of identity, can facilitate self-reflection and allyship among Asian American students that lead to greater racial consciousness and liberatory action.

Challenging our own community members can seem like we are fragmenting or weakening our Asian American movement, but in fact we believe not doing so is what will cause our downfall. Intersectionality can help us critically analyze power and oppression in the full range of our experiences shaped by race and other identities. To courageously and compassionately call in our community members to do better means we have not given up on our community. We believe that liberation is possible and we must live into our values in the very place that is supposed to be our center, our core, our home.

REIMAGINING OUR WORK

Engaging in liberatory practices on campuses in which our values may be out of place can seem like an impossibility. Through the fast-paced, overworked, achievement-oriented culture of student affairs, we have learned to prevent burnout by protecting our personal well-being as sacred. We have found slowing down and sitting in stillness (metaphorically and literally) can be rejuvenating for our emotional, spiritual, physical, and mental health. Lifelong revolutionary Grace Lee Boggs (2012) argues that radical activism is turning inward to do soulwork, the kind of work that nurtures our hearts and spirits so that we can creatively imagine a new world. The following ethics have helped us tend to, heal, and invigorate our souls: love, community, and forgiveness.

For us, love is foundational to social justice work. bell hooks (2001) writes "echoing the work of Erich Fromm, he defines love as 'the will to extend one's self for the purpose of nurturing one's own or another's spiritual growth'" (p. 4) and expands, "when we understand love as the will to nurture our own and another's spiritual growth, it becomes clear that we cannot claim to love if we are hurtful and abusive" (p. 6). While oppression creates violence, bigotry, and hate in our world, practicing love has brought us strength, communion, vulnerability, and deep connection. In particular, the hardest place to start with love for us has been within ourselves *for* ourselves. We have often doubted our abilities, knowledge, and skills. Even now, there are endless workplace pressure points that bring us back to self-doubt. Nonetheless, we believe that self-love is critical to our survival and success in higher education. If we do not learn to love ourselves, then we cannot offer that same love to the students that we serve.

Actively reaching out to community has helped us feel less alone in our work. Oppression operates to sever our connection to others so that we remain divided under the rule of the oppressor. We are socialized to compete with one another and prioritize our self-interest. In higher education, the presumption of scarce resources, the myth of meritocracy, and unaddressed institutionalized racism force us into positions of distrust, competition, and silos. Yet, we have found success in instances when we have reached out to colleagues and faculty for support. Through building and trusting in community, we have connected more deeply with others with whom we have not thought was possible to connect. For us, this connection has included community with Asian Americans and professionals of color who we have not known before and allies of dominant social identities.

Lastly, forgiveness has been an important and tough lesson for us. As social change agents, we have high expectations for ourselves and others to advance a liberatory agenda. Yet, we have made mistakes where we have caused harm to our community members and have also been hurt by others within the community. To be liberated means we allow ourselves to be humans, which includes an understanding that humans make mistakes. For us, forgiveness is about letting go of expectations that we or others should be a certain way. Understanding love as a spiritual growth process means we embrace mistakes and find lessons in each one. Practicing forgiveness for ourselves and others has been critical for our individual and collective healing.

These guiding ethics are an evolving and interlinked framework for us. We hope that Asian American professionals and professionals of color alike can find utility and inspiration within them. We invite all higher education professionals to try on and add to these ethics. We envision a world where we as staff, administrators, and students can all feel free and wholly human, on campus and off. Together we can uplift and support each other in our efforts to cultivate our collective liberation for the present and future generations to come.

REFERENCES

American Council on Education. (1937). *The student personnel point of view* (American Council on Education Studies, series 1, no. 3). Washington, DC: Author.

Boggs, G. L. (2012). Reimagine everything. *Race, Poverty, & the Environment, 19*(2), 44–45.

Crenshaw, K. (1989). Demarginalizing the intersection of race and sex: A black feminist critique of antidiscrimination doctrine, feminist theory, and antiracist politics. *University of Chicago Legal Forum, 1989*(1), 139–167.

hooks, b. (2001) *All about love: New visions.* New York, NY: Perennial.

Jones, S. R., & Stewart, D.-L. (2016). Evolution of student development theory. *New Directions for Student Services, 2016*(154), 17–28.

Kim, J. (2012). Asian American racial identity development theory. In C. L. Wijeyesinghe & B. W. Jackson III (Eds.), *New perspectives on racial identity development* (2nd ed., pp. 138–160). New York, NY: NYU Press.

Kodama, C. M., McEwen, M. K., Liang, C. T. H., & Lee, S. (2002). An Asian American perspective on psychosocial student development theory. *New Directions for Student Services, 97*, 45–59. https://doi.org/10.1002/ss.38

Museus, S. D., & Park, J. J. (2015). The continuing significance of racism in the lives of Asian American college students. *Journal of College Student Development, 56*(6), 551–569.

Omatsu, G. (2010). The "four prisons" and the movements of liberation: Asian American activism from the 1960s to the 1990s. In J. Y. S. Wu & T. C. Chen (Eds.), *Asian American studies now: A critical reader* (pp. 298–330). New Brunswick, NJ: Rutgers University Press.

CONCLUDING THOUGHTS

Lift Every Voice and Sing

Monica Galloway Burke and U. Monique Robinson

The collective voice formed by the narratives in the book is enlightening and powerful. The authors were open and reflective in sharing their experiences and we are sure that some of the shared experiences will resonate with many professionals of color in student affairs. Often, we both found ourselves nodding our heads, saying "Amen," and feeling the emotion and genuineness emanating from their words. Our hope is that anyone who reads their narratives will respect their journey, recognize their tenacity, and feel uplifted.

By cultivating a collective voice, seeds can be planted to sprout awareness and hopefully, those who become aware will then cultivate an environment that truly reflects the diversity, inclusion, and respect that higher education institutions espouse in their mission and vision statements. It is human nature for an individual to desire feeling welcomed and appreciated for their efforts and every human deserves to feel safe in their space. However, as detailed in the narratives, those spaces for professionals of color can be filled with censure, discrimination, bias, stereotypes, filtered expectations, insults, passive aggressiveness, confusion, isolation, disrespect, tokenism, manipulation, and cultural blindness. Fortunately, such unpleasant

No Ways Tired, pages 185–187
Copyright © 2019 by Information Age Publishing
All rights of reproduction in any form reserved.

185

experiences can be tempered or countered through support, knowledge, and development.

The browning of America precipitates the need for more student affairs professionals of color at all levels at colleges and universities. The very presence of professionals of color enhances the lives of students, particularly students of color, and the overall campus climate. Their lived experiences are valid and real and acknowledgement of these experiences by staff of color makes students feel supported and heard.

No Ways Tired endeavors to give voice to the often-marginalized student affairs professionals of color, allowing them the space to be their authentic selves. We spend much of our time pouring into others and giving back and subsequently, as these narratives indicate, self-awareness, self-care, and self-preservation become a critical part of our journey. We must take care of ourselves and each other so the important work we do is sustainable, credible, ever evolving, and relevant.

Insights from the narratives also provide practical strategies to potentially enhance the endurance and career mobility of professionals of color in student affairs. Professionals of color in student affairs should use strategies to develop professionally, engage in self-care, as well as sustain and protect themselves. In addition, they should use reflective analysis and their personal *board of directors'* counsel to recognize when it is time to move on to pursue other opportunities to enhance their professional lives when the situation is emotional harmful. Taking such chances involves intentional efforts to enhance professional growth and marketability and create social capital.

Salient themes for the professionals of color emerged from the narratives as well as perceptible strategies. The themes included:

- Dealing with difficult societal structures such as the "Black Tax—an axiom that refers to how Black people must work harder than their White counterparts to achieve similar outcome; the model minority myth—the view that Asian American and Pacific Islanders are a monolithically hardworking racial group whose high achievement undercuts claims of systemic racism made by other racially minoritized populations within the institutional contexts and double burden—the multifaceted disparities experienced because of the duality of race and their gender.
- Racial and ethnic identity (e.g., Indigenous, African American, Black, Biracial, Multiracial, Latinx, Chicano, and Nigerian American) and gender/sexual identity being linked to the professional identity of professionals of color.
- Self-confidence and self-efficacy being eroded and infiltrated by imposter syndrome and double consciousness.

- Commonly being subjected to the personal responsibility and professional expectation from colleagues to consistently support students of color (e.g., other mothering) and serve as the "diversity guru" when needed, whether in our job description or not.
- Facing and surviving microaggressions and macroaggressions as well as racial battle fatigue while trying to survive and thrive in their personal and professional lives.
- The absence of meritocracy for professionals of color when it comes to opportunities and promotions.
- Marginalization and isolation, which can manifest through subtle or overt actions, impacting the social, emotional, and professional well-being of professionals of color.

Despite the limitations the impediments place on a professional of color's career trajectory and workplace well-being, the authors recommended practical strategies to deal with the structural and psychological obstacles they face and how to flourish as a professional of color. Although there is not a panacea to resolve all issues that professionals of color will encounter in the workplace, some of the noted needs and strategies that we and the authors suggest to survive and thrive in higher education, especially at predominantly white institutions, include:

- Mentorship is truly needed to nurture your professional development, whether it occurs through formal, informal, or electronic means as well as cross-racial, cross-gender, or peer-to-peer.
- Professional support networks of peers, allies, and confidantes, as well as counterspaces, on and off campus, where you can construct and maintain yourself are necessary for equilibrium.
- A social network of family and friends is needed to provide social and emotional support to help mitigate any stressors and uplift you.
- Self-care is needed often, particularly putting yourself first when feeling overwhelmed while trying to balance competing demands of your time and attention. In addition, remember there is nothing wrong with asking for help, including seeking a professional counselor, when in need.
- Engage in self-love as often as possible and know your worth. Sometimes, you may need to set boundaries, protect yourself from toxic people and environments, focus more on what you need rather than want, and forgive yourself when needed. You may also need to remind yourself at times that you are not defined by your job and instead, define yourself by your beliefs, what you love to do, and who you love to be around.

- Self-discovery, self-reflection, and storytelling can be used to create context and legitimize your experiences, decisions, and pathways as well as to rejuvenate yourself.
- Know yourself and be authentic, which can hopefully encourage you to feel empowered, which can help you be the best version of yourself in all roles. "Try on" approaches you believe can work well for you in the work environment, but have an objective understanding of your personality, desires, motives, strengths, and weaknesses. Your actions should be in sync with your values while recognizing if you are instead just trying to please someone else or get something from someone.
- Determine which coping strategies, such as faith and spirituality, can be used as a guide and means to overcome stress and distress. Family and friends can sustain you during troubling times and encourage you whether they understand what you do or not.
- Build your social capital and professional repertoire as necessary for you to connect and grow. For example, learn all you can about your role and field, continue your education, take on new projects, participate in professional development, collaborate outside of your area, and diversify your experiences.
- Develop your transferable skills (e.g., communication, problem solving, planning, teamwork, and time management) to help you be adaptable in any role and marketable.
- Expand yourself, such as getting involved in consulting, publishing, researching, and conducting workshops and webinars, to be innovative and hone another set of skills.
- Learn the system, gain knowledge, and stay informed to help you in analyzing a situation or context and remaining vigilant. Be sure to also observe the politics in your work environment while learning to be politically savvy, which requires you to be socially astute, amicable, persuasive, credible, and sincere. In addition, evaluate what you have learned, and adapt as necessary.
- Avoid participation in divisiveness and "in-fighting" with other professionals of color. No one's light needs to be diminished or eliminated, believing there can be only one at the table, as everyone's light can shine simultaneously.
- Advocate for yourself, reach out, and connect to empower others.
- Recognize when it is time to move on and take your talents elsewhere. Of course, always do your homework first before going to a new institution or organization. Look for an environmental fit where you can contribute, thrive, and continue to grow.

The experiences of the authors can also be used to educate higher education administrators in positions of influence about the needs and barriers for professionals of color and highlight the need to address these issues and instigate change. Such complicated conversations are needed to shift the dynamics that thwart the effectiveness and accomplishments of professionals of color toward equitability and the conferral of opportunities based on merit and relevant and objective criteria. Of course, the communication of unconditional positive regard is a major curative factor in any approach to address the barriers and concerns professionals of color encounter, which consequently gives permission to the professional of color to have their own feelings, experiences, and realities. In the end, it is time for higher education to take a critical look at the experiences of professionals of color in student affairs and although progress does not always move in a straight line, it must happen. Certainly, it is worth critically appraising existing practices and approaches to honor the commitment to diversity espoused by institutions of higher education and implementing steady institutional support structures and policies developed through proactive, long-term planning. In the end, student affairs professionals of color are an undeniable asset to college environments and it is our hope that the narratives start a conversation that leads to action.

Above all, celebrate the small steps as well as the major accomplishments. Doing so can help you stay energized and positive.

ABOUT THE EDITORS

Dr. Monica Galloway Burke is an associate professor in the Department of Counseling and Student Affairs at Western Kentucky University. She earned a Bachelor of Arts degree in psychology from Tougaloo College; a Master of Science degree in counseling psychology from the University of Southern Mississippi; and a Doctor of Philosophy degree in educational administration and supervision with an emphasis in higher education from the University of Southern Mississippi. Prior to her 21 years of experience as a faculty member and practitioner in student affairs and higher education, she worked in the field of mental health.

Dr. Burke's research interests include college student development; professional development; helping and coping skills; and topics related to diversity and societal issues. She has authored numerous peer-reviewed articles in scholarly journals and contributed chapters to various books. Furthermore, she served as the lead author for *Helping Skills for Working With College Students: Applying Counseling Theory to Student Affairs Practice* (Routledge, 2017) and is a co-editor for *No Ways Tired: The Journey for Professionals of Color in Student Affairs*. She also serves as a co-editor for two upcoming books related to higher education professionals working with college students in distress. Additionally, Dr. Burke has conducted over 100 workshops and presentations at the international, national, regional, state, and local levels.

Dr. Burke currently serves and has served on editorial boards of professional journals as a co-editor, associate editor, and reviewer. She also supervised numerous research theses, dissertations, and research projects, some of which led to co-authored published manuscripts with students. Dr. Burke

No Ways Tired, pages 191–192

remains actively involved in professional associations and has consistently held leadership roles in the Southern Association for College Student Affairs (SACSA). In addition, she is committed to service within the campus and local community. Dr. Burke has received recognition and several awards for her commitment to preparing graduate students for a career in student affairs, her efforts and scholarship to promote the field of student affairs, and her work related to diversity in higher education.

Dr. U. Monique Robinson is the assistant dean for Peabody College student affairs at Vanderbilt University, where she is responsible for undergraduate, professional, and online students. She provides undergraduate academic support and is the liaison to campus mental health and wellness resources. Additionally, she oversees various aspects of orientation, retention, and commencement. Prior to Vanderbilt University, she was the director of student life and diversity initiatives at Volunteer State Community College (VSCC) in Gallatin, Tennessee. Now with 28 years in higher education, she began her career as assistant director of Admissions at Nazareth College.

Her educational background includes a Bachelor of Science in studio art from Nazareth College. Monique has a Masters of Education in student personnel services and Doctor of Education in higher education administration, both from Peabody College at Vanderbilt University.

Dr. Robinson, who has been actively engaged in community service, especially related to mentoring, is a member and past officer of the Nashville Metropolitan Alumnae Chapter of Delta Sigma Theta Sorority, Inc. and past local chapter president and national secretary of Societas Docta, Inc. She has volunteered with the NAACP ACT-SO program, served several terms on the National Conference on Race and Ethnicity (NCORE) National Advisory Committee and currently, serves on the board of R.A.C.E. Mentoring. She received VSCC's Outstanding Professional/Administrative Award, the Women in Higher Education in Tennessee (WHET) June Anderson Award, the Association for the Promotion of Campus Activities Leadership Award, and Peabody College's Distinguished College Staff Award, and is a graduate of Vanderbilt Leadership Academy. Most recently, she received the Organization of Black Graduate and Professional Student Distinguished Faculty Award.

ABOUT THE CONTRIBUTORS

DaVida L. Anderson is a PhD candidate in the higher education and student affairs (HESA) program at the University of Iowa. She is founder and executive director of Strong Sister, Silly Sister, Inc., a nonprofit organization (www.strongsistersillysister.org), which is committed to empowering first-year college women to embrace ethical choices and become their best self. DaVida has worked in student affairs in various roles as an administrator, actively serves in numerous professional organizations, and is a motivational speaker (www.davidalanderson.com).

Rodney T. Bates, PhD, the director of graduate student and postdoc retention and support in the Graduate College at the University of Oklahoma. Rodney has been in the field of student affairs for 14 years and also serves as an adjunct faculty in the Department of Clara Luper African and African American Studies and Women's and Gender Studies. Rodney's research focuses on diverse student populations experiences at historically White institutions, as well as on dominant and resistant notions of success in higher education.

Joan Collier, PhD, is the associate director for assessment and research for residence life at Rutgers University, New Brunswick. She is co-founder of #CiteASista a Black feminist digital project that focuses on citational practices that center Black women's work, fosters community for Black women with and beyond the academy, and encourages the development of Black feminist ethics and praxis.

No Ways Tired, pages 193–198
Copyright © 2019 by Information Age Publishing
　　　　　　193

Shirley M. Consuegra, MA, is a transition and retention advocate in the Office of New Student Programs at the University of Rhode Island. Shirley has been in the field of higher education for 17 years. She remains active addressing social justice issues both on campus and in the community.

Araceli Cruz, MA, is an associate director of financial aid at Linfield College. She has 7 years of experience as a higher education professional and serves as the equity, diversity, and inclusion chair for the Oregon Association of Financial Aid Administrators. Araceli serves on various scholarship selection committees, serves on education boards, and local college readiness programs.

John Carl Cruz, MS, is a transition and retention advocate in the Office of New Student Programs at the University of Rhode Island. John has been in the field of higher education for 13 years. He is a member of various on-campus groups focused on inclusive practice.

Dal Dean, PhD is a lecturer in the Department of Education Studies at the University of California–San Diego. He teaches courses and conducts research on the following subject areas: education, diversity, race, and equity and access issues in higher education. Dal is also a member of numerous professional organizations and community groups.

Jude Paul Matias Dizon is a doctoral student and USC provost's fellow in the urban education policy program, Rossier School of Education at the University of Southern California. Jude Paul's research interests include campus racial climate, equity-focused organizational change, and Asian American and Pacific Islander student experiences in higher education.

Frederick V. Engram Jr., MS, is a graduate enrollment management expert. He is also an adjunct faculty member in American University's School of Education. Frederick has been in the field of higher education for 13 years. He has also served on several appointed university committees.

Rocío D. Hernández, EdD, is counseling faculty serving as the counselor and coordinator for the CalWORKs program at Ventura College. Rocío has been in the field of student affairs for over 14 years including her experience as a graduate student. She is a member of both ACPA and NASPA where she has served in various professional volunteer capacities.

Justin Grimes, PhD, is the assistant director for the Office of Recruitment, Diversity, and Inclusion at the Graduate School at Virginia Tech Polytechnic Institute and State University. He has worked in the higher education for over 10 years and his research area focuses on issues of marginalization among graduate students, mentorship opportunities for staff members and students of color, and motivation.

DanaMichelle Harris, MA, is a program administrator at Montclair State University. Dana Michelle has worked in higher education for 16 years and also serves as an adjunct faculty in the First-Year Experience at Montclair State University. She is a PhD candidate in the higher education program at Rutgers University–New Brunswick.

Tennille T. Haynes, MEd, is the director of the Carl A. Fields Center for Equality and Cultural Understanding at Princeton University. Tennille has been in the field of student affairs for 13 years and is currently a PhD student in the higher education program at Rutgers University. Tennille's passion lies in serving as an educator for students and as a resource for faculty and staff on issues of diversity, inclusion, social justice and community.

Karen F. Jackson, EdD, serves as the associate dean for advising programs in the School of Transitional Studies and an assistant professor of Education at Georgia Gwinnett College. She has 25 years' experience in education that includes work in K–12 and higher education institutions. Karen volunteers in her local community and is active in professional organizations.

Melvin (Jai) Jackson, PhD is the director for graduate student recruitment, mentoring, and success for the College of Education at North Carolina State University. Jai has been a dedicated higher education professional for over 10 years and has served at institutions within the United States and abroad. He is actively involved in supporting the future of higher education through training, mentoring, and engaging future professionals.

Kimberly D. Johnson, EdD, is the executive assistant to the chancellor at the University of Missouri–Kansas City. Kimberly served in the field of student affairs for 10 years and is adjunct faculty in the Helzberg School of Management at Rockhurst University in Kansas City. MO. She is a member of numerous campus committees, professional organizations and community groups.

Marvette Lacy, PhD, is the Women's Resource Center director at the University of Wisconsin–Milwaukee. Her research focuses on using critical theories to explore identity development of college women, the dynamics of power and privilege in sexual violence and response movements, and the intersections of race and gender in student activism.

Laila I. McCloud is a doctoral student in the higher education and student affairs (HESA) program at the University of Iowa. Laila's research critically examines issues of race and equity within higher education with a focus on the experiences of minoritized students. She is an active member of the American College Personnel Association (ACPA), the American Educational Research Association (AERA), and the Association for the Study of Higher Education (ASHE).

Sharee L. Myricks is the assistant director of the Passport Office at Indiana University Purdue University Indianapolis & Ivy Tech Coordinated Programs. Sharee has served in multiple positions within academic advising and student services during her eight-year career in student affairs. Sharee is currently a doctoral student researching the resilience of women and social justice within higher education.

Uzoma F. Obidike is an educator with expertise in student activities, leadership development, and career readiness. In addition, she is also the founder of She Leads Beautifully where she helps mid-career professional women advance to the next level. Uzoma serves in various leadership roles in Northwest Indiana and is also pursuing a doctorate in higher education leadership at Indiana State University

Roberto C. Orozco, MS, is a doctoral student in the higher education PhD program at Rutgers University–New Brunswick. He currently serves as the graduate researcher for the Office of Enrollment Management in addition to the Tyler Clementi Center at Rutgers University–New Brunswick. He has over 5 years working in student affairs and higher education with a focus on diversity and social justice initiatives.

Kelli A. Perkins is associate director of residential education at the University of Vermont. Over the last 12 years in the field of student affairs, Kelli has served in roles in residential life, first year experience, orientation, and student leadership & engagement. She is the current Vermont state director for NASPA and is also a doctoral candidate at Northeastern University.

Merylou Rodriguez is the director of scholarships, housing and student engagement at Douglass Residential College in Rutgers University–New Brunswick. Merylou has been in the field of higher education for over 5 years and is current a second year student in the higher education PhD program at the Rutgers Graduate School of New Brunswick.

Allison C. Roman, MSW, is the inaugural director for diversity and inclusion at Trinity University, San Antonio, TX. Allison has previously held positions in multi-cultural affairs and women and gender equity centers. She is the founder of the Women of Color Directors Network, a network for women of color diversity and social justice leaders in higher education.

Cynthia N. Sánchez Gómez is a doctoral student in the Higher Education PhD program at Rutgers University–New Brunswick. Cynthia has been in the field of student affairs for 5+ years and currently serves as a director at the Douglass Project for Rutgers Women in STEM within Douglass Residential College (Rutgers University). Her current research focuses on exploring the unique challenges and obstacles faced by undocumented students attending college.

Ashley Spicer-Runnels, EdD, is an assistant vice provost in the Office of Academic Affairs at Texas A&M University–San Antonio. Ashley has been in the field of higher education for 13 years, serving as administer and adjunct faculty. She is a member of numerous professional organizations and holds multiple leadership positions.

Aaron Slocum is the program coordinator for 21st Century Scholars at Indiana State University. Aaron has been in the field of student affairs for 7 years and has done research focusing on the success of students of color, food insecurity, and living-learning communities.

Richard Song, MS, is the assistant director in the Office of New Student Programs at the University of Rhode Island. Richard has been in the field of higher education for 9 years. He is a member of professional organizations and community groups.

Dantrayl Smith, EdD, serves as the coordinator for the intercultural Student Engagement and Academic Success Network at Tarrant County College in Fort Worth Texas. Dantrayl has been in the field of student affairs for over 10 years and his research area of focus is African American male students and staff in higher education. He is a member of numerous professional organizations and community groups.

Terah J. Stewart PhD, is an assistant professor in the Student Affairs and Higher Education program at Iowa State University. TJ has served in a variety of student affairs roles but has spent most of his time in multicultural affairs engaging equity and justice work. TJ research interests include student activism, resistance, critical theory, fat-body politics, sex work, and the experiences of Black people in the academy.

Michael R. Williams, EdD, is the director of The Gwendolyn Brooks Cultural Center at Western Illinois University. He has served in the realm of higher education for 6 years and has supervised three Male Initiatives Programs at different institutions. Michael has also served on numerous national professional organizations.

rita zhang, MEd, has worked professionally in higher education for over six years and most recently served as an interim director of an affinity-based student resource center at a large public university in California. As a scholar-activist-practitioner, she infuses principles and theories of coalition building, anti-oppression, and community development into her work with students.

Made in the USA
Coppell, TX
03 September 2020